CW00968074

Infinite
Bandwidth

Infinite Bandwidth
Encountering Christ in the Media

Eugene Gan
Foreword by Fr. Mitch Pacwa, S.J.

EMMAUS
ROAD
PUBLISHING

Steubenville, Ohio
A Division of Catholics United for the Faith
www.emmausroad.com

EMMAUS
ROAD
PUBLISHING

Emmaus Road Publishing
827 North Fourth Street
Steubenville, Ohio 43952

©2010 by Eugene Gan
All rights reserved. Published 2010
Printed in United States of America
13   2 3 4

Library of Congress Control Number: 2010934255
ISBN: 978-1-931018-67-8

Scripture quotations are from Revised Standard Version of the Bible—Second Catholic Edition
(Ignatius Edition) Copyright © 2006 National Council of the Churches of Christ in the United
States of America. Used by permission. All rights reserved.

Excerpts from the English translation of the Catechism of the Catholic Church for the United
States of America copyright © 1994, United States Catholic Conference, Inc.—Libreria Editrice
Vaticana. English translation of the Catechism of the Catholic Church: Modifications from the
Editio Typica copyright © 1997, United States Catholic Conference, Inc.—Libreria Editrice
Vaticana. Noted as "CCC" in the text.

Cover design and layout by Julie Davis, General Glyphics, Inc., Dallas, Texas (www.glyphnet.com)

Dedication

To Our Heavenly Father,
through Our Blessed Mother,
Fiat Voluntas Tua!

Table of Contents

Foreword
by Fr. Mitch Pacwa

A series of major changes has occurred during my lifetime in the arena of the mass media. As a small child I listened to a few radio soap operas with my Grandmother, but very soon these stories ceased being broadcast on radio because they moved to television, which was beginning to expand its broadcast time into larger chunks of time early in the day. Chicago was able to receive only four channels—the three national networks and a local station, WGN—though that was more than many cities enjoyed. The screens were small and the colors limited to black, white and gray. As with the soap operas, the formats for TV were drawn from radio and the movies. Video tape would not be available until the early 1960s, so much programming was live and oriented to viewing by any and all members of the family.

Throughout the last half of the twentieth century we were amazed and pleased with technological changes in the media—larger television screens, color, transistor radios, video players and recorders, audio cassette tapes, compact disk players and recorders, DVD players and recorders, computers, laptops, the Internet, cell phones, cable and satellite TV and radio, etc. I still remember seeing the first unveiling of a room-sized computer on the Art Linkletter Show in the mid 1950s. The lighthearted application was an attempt to help match men and women for the perfect marriages through a computer program. Little did we imagine that within forty years we could buy palm size calculators and computers that would outperform Univac.

During my undergrad years at the University of Detroit I became a student of R. Buckminster Fuller, the inventor of the geodesic dome, among other things. His lectures as a visiting professor laid out the general lines of the development of the new technology, including personal computers, cell phones, and satellite television. Still, I never ceased to be amazed at each new technology and its accessibility to the general public at a rapid pace.

This rapid development of the physical tools of the media was accompanied by two significant phenomena: the proliferation of media outlets; and a radical change in cultural values.

From the 1950s until the early twenty-first century the number of nationally available television stations has gone from three to hundreds. The availability of international channels through satellite or through the Internet magnifies the number tremendously. News, sports, and entertainment for every taste and interest can be present in any home with the appropriate technology.

At the same time the culture has gravitated from the Judaeo-Christian family values of the first half of the twentieth century to a relativistic withdrawal from upholding these values. This change occurred over five decades because of a confluence of influences. One influence was the rise of various psychologies to popular consciousness. Some of them, particularly the Freudians, understood sexual repression as the cause of most human suffering. Then, the behaviorists asserted that the human psyche can be quantified and behavior changed without reference to a mythic free will. This school asserted that no moral values could be measured and therefore did not exist. Another school, the existentialists, claimed that human freedom is the touch point of all meaning in life. However, with no other referent to form the basis upon which truth could be built, each person needs to find the core of freedom within and then define whatever meaning appears best.

Besides these intellectual movements, a variety of popular movements swept not only America but many other regions of the world. Among them were the wider use of various illegal drugs, which has become so rampant and whose distribution system is so violent that strong moves for legalization of these drugs have taken hold of some European nations and some American states. Another popular movement has been the widespread acceptance of sex outside of marriage. Now some nations and states have redefined marriage beyond the one man, one woman and children model.

While experimentation with sexual and drug use may not require too much encouragement among many segments of society, for the sake of the rest of the people a type of justification has been based on an insistence on a relativistic morality. The very existence of such diverse "lifestyles" means that no one has the authority or even ability to determine society's moral norms. Cultural leaders exhort all people to stop judging others, not because of Jesus Christ's admonition to humbly avoid declarations of God's eternal judgment on other persons, but because no basis exists to judge whether behaviors are good or bad. Relativism makes it difficult to prohibit the violent, the pornographic, or the philosophically cynical attitudes that are opposed to truth and beauty.

Of course, these changes in philosophy, psychology, and relativistic morals have made their presence known quite forcefully on television. Television has moved from Lucy and Ricky (and every other television married couple) sleeping in separate beds to any and every sexual act being easily available for viewing by anyone who desires it. Television fathers moved from being wise and caring men who respected their wives and children (e.g., Father Knows Best) to dolts who cannot stop or even criticize their wives' or children's licentious behavior.

Despite this moral decline, the desire for truth cannot be completely suppressed by society's emerging or dominant lack of traditional values. An essential component of being human is the possession of reason and memory, by which knowledge is thoughtfully considered and decisions are made. The ability to think well continues to emerge as many media offer alternatives to the dominant relativism. There are many religious networks, educational channels, political and economic networks. Though this diversity may seem minuscule compared to the outlets available on cable television or the Internet, it remains available and the opportunities to make it grow are also available.

How will people negotiate their way through the media? Some of it is horribly wicked (to make a bold judgment), some is naughty, much is mediocre or silly, and some of it is quite good. How do we decide which is virtuous and which leads to vice? What guidance can we find in order to direct our way through the media?

The Catholic Church has always understood itself as a spiritual and moral guide, not only for Catholics but for all people of good will. Not only does the Church draw from revelation in Sacred Scripture and Sacred Tradition, but she invites careful thinking based on application of the natural law to all new circumstances. Naturally, many elements of society fear the Church itself, particularly its authority to condemn bad behavior and to promote the good. They do not want censorship, since it contradicts the dominant culture's relativism. The critics of the Church and her critiques maintain a naive optimism that everyone is so basically good that no harm can arise from giving permission to broadcast or publish any and all ideas. Of course, such naiveté forgets or ignores the damage done by many evil ideas from ancient times until the present—racism, nationalism, and that horribly dangerous denial of God's existence by atheists. Proof can be derived from a consideration of the successful use of the media that prepared the way for the widespread violence perpetrated by Lenin, Stalin, Hitler, Tojo, Mao Tse Dung, Pol Pot, and others. In fact, the perpetrators of mass destruction of life became quite adept at manipulating the media to promote their ideas and to hide their misdeeds.

The Catholic Church is not naively optimistic about humanity. But she is filled with hope for all persons. She recognizes that human nature is fallen; people are born sinners whose concupiscence distorts any and every good creature made by God our Lord. They usually distort the good because of selfish desires that are combined with fear and ignorance. The Church's response to the persistence of sin throughout history is not to throw up her hands in despair and condemnation that people have not changed yet. Rather, she teaches as much of the truth of God that she knows, and she offers various means of grace which God has given her in the sacraments, Sacred Scripture, the wisdom of the Magisterium, and her sacramentals.

Like a bright beam from the old medium of the lighthouse, the Church has poured light upon the media and its uses. As is true of any other light shining in the darkness, human eyes must adjust themselves to the brightness in order to see other objects clearly and usefully. Dr. Gan here offers us a tool to adjust our minds to understand the Church's broad, yet little known, teaching on the media and its content. He has focused the Church's many documents into seven organizing principles. This book is not merely meant to protect us from the media's shoals and reefs that can shipwreck our spiritual, moral, and mental lives. This book helps us become leaders who can guide the whole of our society into the safe and quite beneficial media harbors where our faith and morals, our intellectual and cultural development, and our ability to have fun and economic growth can truly prosper.

Preface

Writing a book about media is, in many ways, like shooting a moving target. Technology changes so rapidly, and the media that consumes the culture one day is often forgotten about the next.

In *Communio et Progressio*, the Second Vatican Council's pastoral instruction on social communication, the Church acknowledged this problem, noting that its document, "sets out basic doctrinal principles and general pastoral guidelines. It carefully refrains from going into minute details on a subject which is continually changing and developing and which varies so much according to time and place." *

I have only been half so wise.

The primary aim of this book, like *Communio et Progressio*, is to lay out the basic principles that, according to the Church's Magisterium and Sacred Scripture, should govern Catholics' understanding and use of the media. And by media, I mean the media of the electronic age.

The term, as used in this book, encompasses all modes of media that rely upon technology and are prevalent in this particular period: movies, radio, TV, CDs, DVDs, videos, the Internet, cell phones, computer/video game consoles, PDAs, and portable media devices, as well as computer programs and applications.

---

* Pontifical Council for Social Communications, Second Vatican Council's Pastoral Instruction on the Means of Social Communication *Communio et Progressio* (May 23, 1971), 3. Available at www.vatican. va/roman_curia/pontifical_councils/pccs/ (hereafter cited in text as CP).

What the term doesn't mean, however, is people. Although we commonly refer to reporters or news producers or film directors as "the media," the term as it's used here refers to their tools and their creations, not the persons themselves. That's an important distinction to keep in mind as you read this book.

It's also important to keep in mind what I said about shooting moving targets. Unlike the Vatican, I've chosen to talk about specific media and media applications in order to illustrate the principles and guidelines presented. To avoid dating the book I've tried to choose a cross section of examples from many decades. But, because we are all creatures of our times and because most of us face specific challenges presented by specific pieces of media right now, many examples are current to the date of this book's publication.

Accordingly, if everyone's favorite social networking site changes three months after this book's publication, I ask for your forbearance with what may seem like old-fashioned or outdated examples. Just keep reminding yourself, "Moving target."

For their help in producing this shooting expedition, I would like to thank my exemplary editor, Emily Stimpson, who made certain that I stayed on target; Mike Aquilina, Shannon Minch-Hughes, and Emmaus Road Publishing for their belief in the importance of this work; and colleagues, friends, and students at Franciscan University of Steubenville for their support. I also owe my thanks to Gary Shank, Doug Lowry, David Carbonara, Randy and Lisa Koslosky, Antonio Soave, Paul Runge, and my parents George and Emilie, for their faith and prayers.

Of course, this book could not have been completed without my lovely and loving wife, Cindy Marie, who kept reminding our boys John Paul, Maximilian Kolbe, and Benedict that Daddy couldn't play with them while he was researching and writing. And guiding my aim through all the study and work was Our Heavenly Father, to whom I am so very grateful, and our Blessed Mother, through whom all has been consecrated.

Googling with God

A Catholic Approach to Media

What does media have to do with faith?

Probably more than you think. And definitely more than most of my students think when they first walk into my classroom.

Don't get me wrong—I love my students. They're my brothers and sisters in Christ. They're also bright, talented, and eager to use media as a means of spreading the Faith. In fact, many of them already do just that. If you check out Proud2BCatholic.com, a website featuring multimedia content developed by Franciscan University of Steubenville students, you'll see dozens of examples of their work—smart, funny, and poignant videos about God, the saints, and Catholic life.

When it comes to evangelizing, my students understand the power and potential of the media. They want to use it to present truth, reveal beauty, and move people to faith, hope, and love. They see the relationship between technology and faith when it comes to the media they *make*. They get it.

But what many don't get, at least not when they first arrive at Franciscan University, is the relationship between faith and the media they *use*. They don't know that the Church has something to say about how they should watch movies, surf the Internet, and play video games. They don't realize that their Faith can and should guide their presence on blogs, chat rooms, and social networking sites, or that their Catholicism should shape their text-messaging habits.

My students aren't alone. Few students their age—Catholic or otherwise—approach media with faith as their guide. Instead, the culture and a lifetime of surfing, googling, and gaming shape their habits of use. In part, that's because young people today have never known a world without cell phones and the Internet. They were blogging and using social networking sites when many of their professors, including me, were still in graduate school. At many a college and university, more students than professors know how to put together a multimedia presentation, design a website, even post pictures online. The same holds true in many if not most households across the country. In the world of twenty-first century technology, young people are the digital natives. The rest of us—mere digital immigrants.[1]

That doesn't mean, however, that adults see the connection between faith and technology any more clearly than our children and students do. A lot of us have good instincts. We're not tempted to send 200 text-messages a day or post intimate details about our relationships online. But we're also not sure how to explain to our children why doing those things is a bad idea.

Like our children, we need a clear guide for how to understand and use media. We all need help navigating our way through this beeping, pinging, ringing, wired world of ours.

St. Peter's Seven Media Keys

And that's what this book aims to do. It is a guidebook, a road map of sorts, for Catholics in the digital age. It gives you a foundation from which you can evaluate media and a barometer for gauging just how much the Faith informs your use of media. It does that by laying out a set of principles about the relationship between faith and media, principles that should inform our media use, as well as our childrens' or students' use. There are seven of these principles, and I call them the seven media keys. The term is mine, the principles are not. Credit for them goes to the Catholic Church.

Over the past seventy-five years, the Church has developed a practical philosophy of social communications upon which Catholics can rely in order to use media well and wisely. When lived, that philosophy enables us to see media for the gift that it is. It also enables us to use media as God intended us to use it—as a means of "contributing to authentic human development and helping individuals and peoples be true to their transcendent destiny." *

So what are the principle elements of this philosophy?

First, the Church calls us to both approach and use media with *balance*. She also calls us to be *aware of the attitudes* behind the media we consume and use. She further teaches that all media and all media technology should respect *the dignity of the human person;* be *truth-filled; inspire* people towards the good, the true, and the beautiful; be *skillfully developed*; and be motivated by and rooted in human *experience*.

These seven principles, or keys, are mentioned again and again in the sixty-plus documents on social communications issued by the Church since 1936. But they're not neatly enumerated in any one encyclical or conciliar writing, which is why so many of us have missed them. We've read the documents, but never connected the dots between them. We've grasped some of the philosophy, but not the whole.

Finding the Keys

I say "we" because I don't know how many times I read the Church's documents on social communications before the pattern of seven core principles emerged.

---

* Pontifical Council for Social Communications, *Ethics in Internet* (February 28, 2002), 1. Available at www.vatican.va/roman_curia/pontifical_councils/pccs/ (hereafter cited in text as EI).

As a teacher and media-maker, I spent years wrestling with the question of how Catholics are called to understand and use media. I wanted a practical tool, a concrete framework that I could give to my students, and that I could use myself. I looked for that tool in studies and papers, books, dissertations, and countless analyses of the media. I poured through writings on instructional technology paradigms, theology, Scripture, and educational philosophy. And again and again, I returned to the dozens of documents authored by the popes and pontifical councils. The more I read those documents, the more I saw how they illuminated everything else I read, and eventually, a picture of the seven keys formed.

Once that picture came together, it was surprisingly clear. The framework seemed so obvious, I'm still not sure how I missed it. I'm not sure how so many of us have missed it. The principles, the seven media keys, should be self-evident to anyone with a Catholic worldview. And yet, they're not, perhaps because we're too immersed in the world of media, unable to see the forest for the trees.

Regardless, the principles are there. And I've seen in my students just how helpful and effective they are.

Students who enter my classroom with the same attitude towards media as their peers at other schools, leave with an entirely different attitude. The Church, not the culture, becomes their guide for googling, texting, and blogging. Movies, commercials, music, video games—all those things and more start being filtered through the lens of faith. The students suddenly see media with a bird's eye view. They have perspective and the ability to navigate their way through the digital world without falling down virtual rabbit holes. That perspective sets them free—free to make good media, and free from the bad habits holding so many of us back from using media as God intended us to use it.

Young people need that perspective. We all need that perspective. We all need to learn to use media as God intended us to use it. If not, there's only one alternative: the media will use us.

Unfortunately, in many ways, it already does. Which is why, before we begin exploring the seven media keys, we first need to understand the good, the bad, and the ugly of our media-saturated world. We need to take stock of where we are, so that we can get where we need to go.

Chapter One

The Media Landscape

A Bird's Eye View of Our Digital World

Jessica Logan made a mistake—a terrible, foolish, immature mistake. And she paid for it with her life.

In the spring of 2008, the eighteen-year-old Cincinnati teenager did what, frighteningly, hundreds of thousands of her peers have also done: she took a sexually explicit picture of herself and sent it to her boyfriend's cell phone. In turn, he forwarded the picture to the cell phones of a few hundred of his friends.

Students at seven schools in the Cincinnati area eventually saw the picture, and teasing and insults followed Logan wherever she went. The shame quickly became too much for Logan, and on July 3, 2008, just one month before she was set to leave for college, she hung herself in her parents' home.

Her heartbroken mother, Cynthia Logan, responded to her daughter's death by launching a national campaign against "sexting"—sending sexually suggestive images via cell phone—and persuaded legislators in several states as well as the U.S. House and Senate to introduce bills banning the practice.[2]

Cynthia Logan's response was natural and understandable. Any other parent, whose eyes were brutally opened to the power of something as seemingly innocuous as a cell phone, might do the same. But no law is going to bring Jessica back. And no law can make up for what tens of millions of people, both young and old, don't have: the ability to use technology and social media prudently, wisely, and for the good of themselves and others.

Gifts from God

If human beings were fish, media would be the sea in which we swim. It's everywhere, shaping how we work, how we learn, how we communicate, how we entertain ourselves, and even how we think.

Just consider the numbers.

In 2009, American adults spent an average of eight hours a day in front of a screen—watching television, playing games, or surfing the Web. A robust 79 percent used the Internet, and nine out of ten owned cell phones. Teens spent slightly more time in front of screens than their parents (8.5 hours), with more of them using the Internet (93 percent) and spending more time there than adults (31 hours per week vs. 14 hours per week). Teen cell phone use has also risen, with 58 percent of twelve-year-olds and 83 percent of seventeen-year-olds owning a mobile phone. Similarly, 77 percent of teens live in homes that own some form of gaming device, while 74 percent own an iPod or mp3 player. [3]

Media and media technology are unquestionably everywhere. But that's not necessarily a bad thing. When used rightly, media can do an untold amount of good.

Thanks to media technology, parents in Singapore can make calls for free over the Internet to their son and grandsons in Pittsburgh. A woman in Washington can show photos of her children to her sisters in Ohio and Michigan through Facebook. Men and women in Iran can share their fight for freedom with the world via micro-blogging platforms such as Twitter. Aid to disaster afflicted third-world countries can pour in from around the globe after CNN broadcasts pictures of their plight, while perfect strangers can become friends as they debate salvation, damnation, and *Lost* in online forums at ABC.com. All those things can happen and do happen. So do countless other acts of communication, charity, and information sharing. Stories of how media technology has brought individuals and nations together could, quite literally, fill an entire library.

For that matter, the Internet itself is a veritable library, with thousands of years' worth of history, literature, and wisdom available in seconds to a savvy Google user. Broadcast, print, and online news keep citizens up-to-date on the workings of their government, while YouTube allows educators not just to tell their students about Martin Luther King Jr.'s "I Have a Dream Speech," but actually to show it to them. Podcasts and blogs also allow individuals to speak their minds on world events and reshape the news cycle, decentralizing determinations about what is and is not important to the masses.

Sacred knowledge can be spread just as effectively as secular knowledge, with Catholics and Baptists debating the place of the sacraments in the economy of salvation on Facebook, poor seminarians in Africa downloading free Bible studies off SalvationHistory.com, and answers to questions about the Faith easily searchable at apologetics websites hosted by Catholics United for the Faith or Catholic Answers. Parishes and dioceses can likewise use their websites to direct their members to sound faith formation resources, while the Vatican makes centuries of papal writings and pronouncements available to anyone who has the desire to look at Vatican.va.

For very good reason, the Catholic Church has called media technologies "gifts from God." * They are tools that can and have been used to connect us, enlighten us, and transform us.

But, like all gifts from God, these tools also can and have been misused.

---

* Pope Pius XII, Encyclical Letter *Miranda Prorsus* (September 8, 1957), 1. Available at http://www.vatican.va/holy_father/pius_xii (hereafter cited in text as MP).

Media and the Digital Natives

The case of Jessica Logan is an extreme example, but not an isolated one. For all their media savvy, many of today's young people fail to grasp what it means to use media wisely. And that failure is doing some serious damage.

At the extreme end of the spectrum, it's damaging the 22 percent of teenage girls—that's one in five—who admit to "sexting" or posting sexually explicit pictures of themselves online. It's also wreaking havoc on the 42 percent of children between the ages of 10 and 17 who admit to viewing online pornography.[4]

Virtually all children have likewise been fed a steady diet of sex and violence through their families' television sets. The number of sexual scenes on TV doubled between 1998 and 2005, and the most recent numbers from the Kaiser Foundation indicate that 70 percent of all television shows include some sexual content, with the average show featuring five sexual scenes per hour. Other studies have concluded that by the time a child finishes elementary school he will have seen 8,000 different murders committed on television and in the movies. By the time he reaches college, the total acts of violence viewed as "entertainment" will have reached 200,000.[5]

Those images of sex and violence don't pass through children's minds without affecting them. Not only does viewing pornography diminish young women's self-respect, but it also contributes to teens' "recreational" view of sex, leading many to see sexual activity as just another bodily function, something akin to eating or drinking. Watching sexual content on television has also been shown to hasten sexual activity in teens, while similar research has demonstrated that exposure to violence on television increases the likelihood of young boys initiating fights. Likewise, men who watched a significant amount of violence on television as children are considered more likely to abuse their wives or girlfriends.[6]

Performance Anxiety

To a lesser extent, improper media use has also contributed to problems in America's classrooms. Despite the billions of additional funds we've invested in our schools in recent years—including billions specifically designated for instructional technology—America's students still aren't making the grade.

Pick a study, any study—the National Assessment of Educational Progress (NAEP), the National Survey of Student Engagement, the Kaiser Family Foundation Program for the Study of Media and Health, the Intercollegiate Studies Institute civic literacy surveys, studies by the National Bureau of Labor Statistics, the National Endowment for the Arts, the National Geographic Society. They all come to the same conclusion: Teens' technological proficiency isn't improving their test scores.

One of those studies, the 2005 NAEP test, reported that 53 percent of American twelfth graders scored "below basic" in history, 46 percent scored "below basic" in science, and 27 percent scored "below basic" on literary tests—all results comparable to or worse than those from similar tests administered in 2003, 2001, and 1994.[7]

Even grimmer is the conclusion reached in the May 2007 ACT report, "Rigor at Risk: Reaffirming Quality in High School Core Curriculum," which asserted that "three out of four ACT-tested 2006 high school graduates...are not prepared to take credit-bearing entry level college courses with a reasonable chance of succeeding..."[8]

Along with falling test scores, teachers and employers have reported a marked decline in young people's ability to research information, assess a source's point of view, write well, and frame an argument. Those reports were confirmed by a 2006 study conducted by the Educational Testing Service, which concluded that out of the 6,300 students tested only a "few" demonstrated strong Information and Communications Literacy Skills.[9]

Bad Habits

Media itself isn't to blame for any of those problems. Cell phones don't force young girls to send illicit pictures of themselves into cyberspace any more than computers make us stupid. Plenty of studies, such as those reported in Steven Johnson's book *Everything Bad is Good for You: How Today's Popular Culture is Actually Making Us Smarter*, have demonstrated that media technology can actually increase mental flexibility and problem-solving abilities.

So, what is to blame?

At least part of the answer seems to lie in how teens use technology.

A 2009 study by a British research group found that teenagers spend an average of 31 hours per week online. That broke down to 3.5 hours instant messaging their friends; 2 hours on YouTube; 3 hours looking for homework help; 9 hours on social network sites; 1 hour looking for weight loss or beauty tips; 1 hour and 40 minutes viewing pornography; and 1 hour and 40 minutes downloading music.[10]

In other words, most teens use technology for what most teens care about: other teens and themselves.

Young people also aren't confining themselves to looking at just one website or YouTube video at a time.

In 2008, Mark Edmunson, a professor at the University of Virginia, recounted in the *Chronicle of Higher Education* how, at least mentally, his students are almost never in one "place." After conducting a survey of UVA undergraduates, Edmunson found that his students actually inhabited an average of seven "places" at once—a feat accomplished by working on a paper, watching a movie, instant messaging with friends, listening to music, visiting various websites, chatting with people in the room, and checking email, all virtually at the same time.[11]

Those habits of use translate into real problems, both morally and intellectually.

Immersed in a universe of fifteen-year-olds, many teens don't recognize the potential of media to do anything other than improve their social standing. They don't see it as a tool to spread the Faith or educate themselves about the Napoleonic Wars. They see it as a tool to talk to their friends, listen to music, and simply be entertained.

In the process, they not only lose out on the other goods media has to offer, but, as Mark Bauerlein argues in his book, *The Dumbest Generation: How the Digital Age Stupefies Young Americans and Jeopardizes Our Future*, they end up drowning out the voices of their parents and teachers with the voices of their peers. They don't hear the voices that teach them right from wrong, introduce them to a world that's bigger than high school, and help them sort through the vast amounts of information coming at them from and through media.[12]

This suggests a reason for why teens do foolish and wrong things like "sexting." Only in a world made up solely of other fifteen-year-olds does a teenage girl think it's a good idea to send pornographic pictures of herself to a teenage boy's cell phone.

It's also in part why test scores are falling. Learning requires concentrated reflection and study. It can't happen when you're studying, listening to music, watching a movie, and instant messaging friends all at the same time. As Edmunson explained, so many students today are "always in motion, always spitting out what comes first to mind, never challenging, checking, revising."[13]

Of course, learning isn't the only thing in life that requires concentrated reflection and study. Spiritual growth requires both. You can't hear God with your iPod blasting. You can't grow in virtue when you spend hours every night playing first person shooter games on your computer.

As one young priest, Father David Marstall of the Diocese of Wichita, recently explained in an interview:

> "Young people today have grown up with Google. They're accustomed to asking questions and finding answers quickly. But when they get to questions that they can't answer in a few minutes, they give up. And when it comes to the spiritual life, to discerning a vocation or understanding the mysteries of the faith, answers don't come quickly. Conversion is harder for teens today compared to 15 years ago."[14]

If conversion is harder, how much harder is actually living the Faith, being guided by it, and making the hard choices all adults need to make? Those are questions soon to be answered as millions of teens come of age.

Media and the Digital Immigrants

As parents, teachers, and responsible adults, it's our job to try to break through the media cacophony confusing and misleading young people. Unfortunately, many of us are equally confused and misled.

Wedded to our cell phones, we interrupt family meals and outings to take business calls. Tempted by the vice of curiosity—wondering if our former classmates have put on weight or lost their thick head of hair—we waste precious hours seeking out old friends on Facebook or Classmates.com. We also watch shows or movies with little awareness of the messages being presented, and bounce from site to site on the Internet, reading much, but absorbing little. Many of us are drowning in information and growing less and less capable of processing that information, of making sense of it, of using it wisely.

Consider, for example, studies by the University of London, which show that while the Internet may encourage wider or more frequent reading, it does not encourage deeper reading. Their research reveals that most adults rarely read more that two pages of text on the Internet before we follow one of the ubiquitous hyperlinks to wherever it may lead. Even more rarely do we return to the page we left behind.[15]

In July 2008, Nicolas Carr penned an article for *The Atlantic* that asked the question, "Is Google Making Us Stupid?" In the article, Carr confessed:

> Over the past few years I've had an uncomfortable sense that someone, or something, has been tinkering with my brain, remapping the neural circuitry, reprogramming the memory. My mind isn't going—so far as I can tell—but it's changing. I'm not thinking the way I used to think. I can feel it most strongly when I'm reading. Immersing myself in a book or a lengthy article used to be easy. My mind would get caught up in the narrative or the turns of the argument, and I'd spend hours strolling through long stretches of prose. That's rarely the case anymore. Now my concentration often starts to drift after two or three pages. I get fidgety, lose the thread, begin looking for something else to do. I feel as if I'm always dragging my wayward brain back to the text. The deep reading that used to come naturally has become a struggle.

Summing up his experience, Carr concluded, "Once I was a scuba diver in the sea of words. Now I zip along the surface like a guy on a jet ski."[16]

In the weeks and months that followed the publication of Carr's article, a chorus of "Me too's" went up across the Internet, with countless journalists and bloggers weighing in on their own experience of "adult onset ADD." What emerged was a picture of a culture where "zipping along the surface on a jet ski" wasn't simply an apt metaphor for how we read, but also for how we live.

Distracted

Today, most Americans live a fast-paced and "totally connected" life. With our iPhones and Blackberries always at hand, anyone can reach us at anytime via phone, email, or text messaging. We can text while driving, talk on the phone while grocery shopping, and surf the Net while cooking dinner. And we do. Technology has made us masters of multi-tasking.

But just as teens' simultaneous studying and surfing causes problems, so too does our simultaneous carpooling and networking.

As Maggie Jackson asserts in her book *Distracted: The Erosion of Attention and the Coming Dark Age*, some of us are almost multi-tasking ourselves to death. Our "to-do" lists never grow shorter. Our in-boxes never empty. And more and more of us struggle to find the time to do what matters most—pray, read, and spend time with those we love—because we're so busy responding to the demands coming at us via phone and email.[17]

In a September 2009 interview with *Our Sunday Visitor*, Jackson noted that the average American worker switches tasks every three minutes. She then went on to explain:

> Essentially, the way we're living is very reactive. We're always trying to respond to a new interruption—a beep, a ring, a ping—and that's compromising our ability to focus, to plan, and pursue our goals, as well as to build real relationships... We're flooded by information, by choices, and by constant change. That leaves us overloaded, fragmented, and hurried.[18]

A totally connected life, for adults and teens, means no time for silence, no time for contemplation, and no time for the studied reflection that has long been considered necessary for self-knowledge, wisdom, and spiritual growth. It also means continual exposure to ideas and images that can work against all three of those goods.

So what are we to do?

Quo Vadis?

It can be tempting, especially for concerned parents, to disavow media altogether—to throw out our cell phones, chuck our TVs, and ban our teenagers from so much as looking at a computer. But that would be a mistake, and believe it or not, it would also be going against more than seven decades of Catholic teaching on media.

Surprised?

In 1936, well before most people in the world even knew what a television set was, let alone owned one, the Church issued her first document on social communications, *Vigilante Cura*. In the years since, more than sixty other major documents have followed. And the message preached by each and every one is that the tools of social communication, media, are "gifts from God," "marvelous things" that "provide some of the most effective means for the cultivation of [charity] among men." The only feast day stipulated by Vatican II was World Communications Day, and the last public document issued by Pope John Paul II was "The Rapid Development," an apostolic letter focused on media and media technologies written in-between hospital visits in early 2005.†

In that document, the pope urged Catholics, "Do not be afraid of new technologies! These rank 'among the marvelous things'—*inter mirifica*—which God has placed at our disposal to discover, to use, and to make known the truth, also the truth about our dignity and about our destiny as his children, heirs of his eternal Kingdom."‡

Early on in the letter, the pope repeated a phrase he first used in his encyclical *Redemptoris Missio*, a phrase in which he compared media to the Areopagus—the social and intellectual hub of ancient Athens—where Paul preached to the pagans.

---

† MP 1; Pope Paul VI, Decree on Media of Social Communications *Inter Mirifica* (December 4, 1963). Available at http://www.vatican.va/archive/hist_councils/ii_vatican_council (hereafter cited in text as IM); CP 12.

‡ John Paul II, Apostolic Letter to Those Responsible for Social Communications *The Rapid Development* (January 24, 2005), 14. Available at www.vatican.va/holy_father/john_paul_ii/apost_letters (hereafter cited in text as RD).

In the eyes of John Paul II, media is the Areopagus of today, the place where Catholics are called to go and engage the culture so that it might come to know and be transformed by Christ (RD 3). And in the eyes of the Church, that's a call Catholics can't neglect. Neglecting it means neglecting the billions of people whose lives are shaped by media. It means neglecting the commission entrusted to us by Christ at His Ascension: go and make disciples of all men.

We can't make disciples of all men unless we go where those men are— unless we speak their language, understand how they think, and know how to respond to their unmet needs. We can't engage the culture if we refuse to enter into the modern day Areopagus and use the tools God has given us to make truth known and serve mankind. We also can't teach our children and students to do the same, let alone protect them from the dangers that media use in our culture inevitably presents.

Those are the reasons behind the Church's clarion call for Catholic engagement in the world of media. Those are also the reasons behind the seven media keys. The Church has given us these keys to educate us and equip us to use media in the right ways and for the right ends. The keys are intended to be a guide for Catholic media engagement, and that engagement begins with balance.

Questions to Ask: My Media Landscape

To understand how media has changed your own world, ask yourself:

1. How many hours a day do I spend in front of the screen of a television, computer, or hand-held device?
2. How many of those hours are for work use? How many are for personal use?
3. How has media brought me closer to others?
4. How has media contributed to problems in my relationships with others?

5. How has media expanded my depth and breadth of knowledge?

6. Has media in any way interfered with how I learn or how I do my job?

7. Do I use media to grow in my faith? If so, how?

8. Am I ever distracted by media? If so, how?

9. Has my own use of media ever put me in any potentially dangerous situations? If so, how?

10. What is my attitude towards media? Do I welcome it or reject it unthinkingly?

Chapter Two

Balance

The First Media Key

They call it "The View," and for good reason.

Situated on the forty-eighth floor of the Marriot Marquis Hotel in New York City's Times Square, The View Restaurant offers patrons a 360-degree look at the Manhattan skyline. Not only do wall-to-wall windows flank all sides of the circular restaurant, but the restaurant itself sits atop a broad revolving platform, something akin to a giant turntable. As people sit at their tables, enjoying braised duck, sautéed scallops, and pumpkin brulee, they also get to see the Big Apple from every possible angle, taking in views of the Hudson River, the Chrysler Building, and Rockefeller Center all in the span of an hour.

The View is an apt symbol of the first media key: balance. In essence, balance is about us. It's about our attitude towards media, our approach to technology. It serves as the foundation for all the other keys because it's the most fundamental mindset we need to cultivate in order to use media wisely.

That mindset, like the restaurant in Manhattan, requires that we look at media from all angles. It calls us to base our understanding of the media we use on careful thought and research. It also calls us to evaluate our own habits of use with the same critical eye.

Perhaps the most concise explanation of what the key of balance requires comes from *Inter Mirifica* ("Among Marvelous Things"), the Second Vatican Council's Decree on the Media of Social Communications. Offering guidance to all those who use and consume media, the Council wrote:

> They must look, then, to the nature of what is communicated, given the special character of each of these media. At the same time they must take into consideration the entire situation or circumstances, namely, the persons, place, time and other conditions under which communication takes place and which can affect or totally change its propriety (IM 4).

Let's break that down, starting with how we evaluate the media we use.

The 360° Exterior View: Understanding Balanced Use

How do we know what movies, games, and gadgets are right for us and for our children? How do we judge the merits of a film or assess the accuracy of a news source? How do we weigh the potential good versus the potential harm of any given piece of media?

It all starts with balance. Without balance, without a willingness to look at media from every possible angle, we can't possibly form right judgments. We run the risk of bias, narrow-mindedness, and ultimately, ignorance.

The phrase, "Keep an open mind," has, for good reason, earned a bad rap with many Catholics. All too often, it comes from the mouths of relativists, trying to dissuade us from believing or asserting some objective truth. What they're really saying, however, is not "Keep an open mind," but rather, "Don't form any opinion whatsoever...unless it happens to be mine."

That's a problem. But being open to new ideas, new points of view, and new possibilities is not. That's how we correct ill-informed opinions, come to right judgments, and learn how to back up our beliefs with reason.

With that being said, when it comes to our initial evaluation of media, we very much need to keep an open mind. We can't judge whether something is good or bad, right or wrong if we're not willing to consider "the entire situation or circumstances."

To a certain extent, this is what Clint Eastwood did when he made the films *Flags of Our Fathers* and *Letters to Iwo Jima*. The first movie told the story of the battle of Iwo Jima from the perspective of the American soldiers who famously raised the stars and stripes over the Japanese island. The second told the same story, recounting the same battle, but from the perspective of the Japanese soldiers.

Eastwood knew that if he wanted to capture the truth about the Battle of Iwo Jima, he couldn't just tell one side's story. He had to tell both. Only by looking at the struggle from all angles could truth emerge.

Most of us aren't filmmakers, but our attitude towards media needs to be the same. We can't approach it simplistically. We can't believe a film is good just because it takes home fifteen Oscars, any more than we can sign off on our twelve-year-old using Facebook simply because all his friends use it. Likewise, we can't write off a film because it might contain some violence or pronounce text-messaging anathema because some people misuse it. We have to be willing to look at more than one viewpoint so that truth can emerge.

To do this, we need to follow *Inter Mirifica's* instructions and take all things into consideration. We have to look at the target audience, the media-maker's intent, the context of certain actions or decisions, and the consequences those actions and decisions bring in order to determine if the media is acceptable for us or for our children. By looking at the media from all angles, we're able to make distinctions that might otherwise elude us.

A Measured Approach: Illustrating a Balanced View

Consider, for example, another film about the Second World War, Steven Spielberg's *Saving Private Ryan*. Love it or hate it, the first fifteen minutes of *Saving Private Ryan* rank among the most violent fifteen minutes on film. They might not have contained as much blood as *Nightmare on Elm Street* and its many sequels, but it was close. So what sets the two apart? Can the one be acceptable viewing and the other not?

Definitely. And here's why.

To start with, there's the question of context. The violence in Spielberg's film takes place in the context of the Allied invasion of Normandy. It has to be there—at least in any realistic depiction of what took place on Omaha Beach. Soldiers on both sides died violent and cruel deaths that day. That's history. The violence in the *Nightmare* movies, however, had no such context to justify it. It wasn't merely gratuitous, it was actually the purpose of the film. The movie was about horror and gore. It was made to showcase grisly "torture porn."[19]

Next, there's the question of presentation. *Saving Private Ryan* begins fifty years after the battle on Omaha Beach, with the first scene depicting one of the soldiers, now an old man, breaking down in tears at a comrade's grave. Those tears set the stage for the tragedy that follows, with the film then moving directly into the scene of the battle, but with no soundtrack to mask the sounds of gunfire and screaming. The presentation is raw, graphic, visceral, but it in no way glorifies bloodshed; it laments it. The message throughout the scene is clear: violence is a nightmare, bloodshed a tragedy. There was no such message in *Freddy vs. Jason*. Instead, indulgent and unnecessary shots of blood and body parts, partnered with a techno-metal soundtrack, boldly proclaim something entirely different: violence is entertainment, bloodshed a pleasure.

Finally, there's intent or purpose. The blood in *Saving Private Ryan* was intended to move viewers to a deeper awareness of our soldiers' sacrifice. On film, as in life, with German guns perched high atop the Norman cliffs, it's evident that the soldiers knew they were on a near-suicide mission. And yet they went anyway. And even as their fellow soldiers lost arms, legs, and heads, as bodies exploded into flames, and boy after boy fell to sniper fire, they still continued up the beach. Watching their slow, bloody progress is brutal, but the theme of heroic sacrifice and bravery is clear. None of the *Nightmare* films had such noble purpose. The blood was never there to inspire gratitude, admiration, and sorrow, but rather to shock, titillate, and terrify.

In addition to considering what takes place on screen and why, the key of balance also calls us to pay attention to who watches those screens. In other words, audience matters. You probably don't want to show *Saving Private Ryan* to your five-year-old, but it's not aimed at five-year-olds. Its target audience is mature adults, an audience that can determine for itself if it can handle the violence. The same can't be said of *Nightmare*. You definitely don't want to introduce a sixteen-year-old to Freddy, and yet that's exactly who the filmmakers want introduced. They made the movie for young people. *Saving Private Ryan* is appropriate for its target audience. The *Nightmare on Elm Street* films are not.

Those are the kind of distinctions that emerge when we look at media from all angles. Rather than issuing blank condemnations of something based on general categories such as "contains violence," we're able to see when a piece of media that contains violence or some level of sexuality might be appropriate, and when it most definitely is not.

A similar kind of analysis helps us determine if we want our children using a certain social networking site or if we should go ahead and purchase an unlimited texting plan.

Remember, technology is a tool. In and of itself, it's neutral. It can, however, be used for good or for ill. Some teenagers use social networking sites to post dangerously inappropriate content online. Others use it to evangelize their classmates. Some men and women text message so much they've forgotten how to carry on a conversation with a person in the same room. Others rely on text messaging to communicate important information that couldn't otherwise be communicated.

We need to take all those possibilities into consideration, along with our own and our children's individual strengths and weaknesses, before we view, use, or continue to use particular forms of media. That's what having a balanced view requires.

The 360° Interior View: Understanding Balanced Use

In *Communio et Progressio*, the Church noted that media consumers:

> "should exercise self-control. They must not allow themselves to be so beguiled by the charms of the media's products or by the curiosity that these arouse that they neglect urgent duties or simply waste time" (CP 52).

Most of us know all too well the kind of beguilement and curiosity of which that document speaks. It's so easy, when sitting in front of a computer all day for work, to stray from the task at hand. The Drudge Report may have posted some scintillating new story. An interesting new blog post could be up in "The Corner." Then there's that new YouTube video that everyone has been talking about. The number of potential distractions on the World Wide Web is, almost literally, endless.

What's true at work is equally true at home. It's so darned tempting to watch just one more episode of *House Hunters* on HGTV, play one more round of *Guitar Hero* on the PlayStation, or post yet another status update on Facebook. It's almost as tempting to run out and buy the latest and greatest version of Nintendo, Kindle, or whatever wonder device Apple has most recently unveiled, confirmed in our belief that a new piece of technology will somehow make our lives better.

With their parents so easily distracted by technology, is it any wonder that children and teenagers are as well? On average, thirty-one hours of their lives each week are spent online. That's more than most parents sleep. And, judging by the numbers, if teens aren't online, they're text messaging. In 2009, teens sent an average of 2,899 text messages a month. That's more than 96 a day. And that's just the average.[20]

Finding Our Balance: Illustrating Balanced Use

It's easy to see what imbalanced use of media looks like. Sending close to 3,000 text messages a month is the perfect picture of that. But what does balanced use of the media look like?

It looks like a healthy diet.

Think of it this way. Chocolate cake and bacon are good things—very good things even. But reason tells us we can't subsist solely on them. We have to eat fish, brussels sprouts, and oatmeal as well. There are also times when our Faith tells us we should consider fasting from good things like chocolate and bacon, times such as Lent and Fridays. Occasionally, we even have to fast from oatmeal and brussels sprouts, forgoing food almost entirely on days such as Ash Wednesday and Good Friday.

That's what eating right looks like: a little bit of everything, more of what's good for us than what's bad for us, and the occasional fast to prevent food from becoming more important than it ought to be.

The same holds true for media consumption. As long as it's not morally problematic, it's okay to consume a little bit of everything. We can play the occasional video game, post the occasional status update, and send the occasional text-message. But we can't just play video games and send text messages. We also need to read the news, talk with friends, and devote time to prayer. Likewise, we need to spend more time reading, talking, and praying than we spend playing *Guitar Hero* or *Mass Effect,* and more time using media to learn about genocide in Darfur or the First Crusade, than about Jennifer Aniston's plastic surgery.

That's essentially what the Church tells us in *Communio et Progressio*, writing, "A proper balance must be kept, not only between hard news, educational material, and entertainment, but also between the light and more serious forms of entertainment" (CP 16).

Keeping that balance likewise requires that from time to time we go on a media fast, abstaining completely from some or all forms of technology. The practice of a media fast is particularly important to maintaining balance. Media, like food, is good. But if we let our need for it control us, it becomes not good. Fasting from media is a way to keep us, not media, in control.

The Church recommended this type of fast in a 1986 document on the training of priests in the use of social media, advising that while abstaining from media use, "students should be guided to the love and practice of reading, study, silence and meditation. They should be encouraged, and be provided with the necessary conditions for community dialogue and prayer." *

During our own periods of fasting from media, we would be wise to do likewise.

Ultimately, practicing the key of balance requires right priorities. As adults, we need to get our priorities straight. We have to ask ourselves what is more important: getting in one more call to our client even though we're in the middle of driving carpool or getting our kids home safely? Reading that article on Drudge or talking with our spouse? Watching reruns of *What Not to Wear* or spending time with God in Eucharistic adoration?

---

* Congregation for Catholic Education, *Guide to the Training of Future Priests Concerning the Instruments of Social Communication* (March 19, 1986), 19. Available at http://www.vatican.va/ roman_curia/pontifical_councils/pccs/ (hereafter cited in text as TFP).

As Christians, we have to order our lives so that we're investing the most time and the most energy in the people and activities that will help us faithfully live out our vocation and grow in holiness. Hence Scripture's admonition: "Do not lay up for yourselves treasures on earth, where moth and rust consume and where thieves break in and steal" (Mt. 6:19). And again, "For where your treasure is, there will your heart be also" (Lk. 12:34). Those words apply to our use of the media as well. We have to order our media use so that it conforms to those goals. Holiness, not *Halo*, must always come first.

Getting the Most Out of Media: Why Balance Matters

Again, the key of balance is the foundation upon which our entire approach to media rests.

By keeping an open mind about media and looking at it from all angles, we can have more informed and balanced opinions. We don't run the risk of missing out on great films such as *Saving Private Ryan* simply because they don't conform to preconceived notions about what is and is not acceptable viewing for Catholics. We also don't miss out on all the social and intellectual benefits some media tools can provide. And we don't undermine our own credibility with others by unthinkingly rejecting that which they believe to be good.

Essentially, the Church tells us that a balanced view of the media enables us to "not only understand the form proper to each of the arts, but also...practice mature consideration and judgment on the various items which the film or television screen puts before them, and not, as very frequently happens, be lured and arbitrarily swept away by the power of their attraction"(TFP 59).

That's what a balanced view of media offers us. But what about balanced use of the media?

Balanced use is the antidote to the dangers of unbalanced use. And those dangers are legion.

Consider the 2008 meta-study conducted by researchers at the National Institutes of Health, Yale University, and California Pacific Medical Center. Looking at all the studies conducted on media use since 1980, these researchers found that 80 percent suggest a close link between too much "screen time" and multiple behavioral and health problems, with tobacco use, sexual promiscuity, obesity, academic performance, and drug and alcohol use all rising in proportion to the number of hours spent in front of a screen.[21]

Then there's the growing problem of Internet addiction. Diagnosed for the first time in 1995, the Center for Internet Addiction asserts that one in eight Americans use the Internet at least somewhat obsessively. Estimates are even higher for China, Taiwan, and Korea. There, studies indicate that nearly one in three |struggle with Internet addiction. China has actually gone so far as to open camps to help Internet addicts break their habit and go through virtual detox in a safe environment.[22]

Now, not everyone who logs on to their computers a little too frequently is going to wind up in some Chinese detox camp. But that doesn't mean there aren't lesser ills from which we all can suffer.

Without applying the first media key to our own use of the media, we usually end up getting less work done, and when we do work, we work less effectively, with the pinging and ringing of email and cell phones perpetually pulling our focus away from where it needs to be. Remember that statistic from the first chapter: the average worker is interrupted every three minutes. That's not exactly a recipe for productivity.

When we're not working, we can also end up wasting precious hours on social networking sites that could be spent with our families, as well as wasting precious dollars on technology upgrades that we don't really need. Likewise, the more time we spend online, playing video games, or watching television, the more likely we are to encounter content that we have no business encountering (i.e. gratuitously violent or sexually explicit material). We also can end up using media for too narrow a purpose—seeing it purely as a tool for entertainment or casual communication, and missing out on all the ways it can help us educate ourselves, be active citizens, and spread the Good News.

There really is so much we can gain from the media, but if we don't approach it with balance, there's also much we can lose.

Applying the First Media Key

STEP 1: PRAY

Pray for the cardinal virtue of temperance, which is necessary for practicing the key of balance.

According to the *Catechism of the Catholic Church*, "Temperance is the moral virtue that moderates the attraction of pleasures and provides balance in the use of created goods. It ensures the will's mastery over instincts and keeps desires within the limits of what is honorable. The temperate person directs the sensitive appetites toward what is good and maintains a healthy discretion" (CCC 1809).

STEP 2: RESEARCH

The next step to applying the key of balance to our use of the media is research. Ideally, before we watch a movie, buy a video game, or invest our time in an online community, we should do our homework.

For some movies or games, a trailer or a preview may be all we need to see before we know if the media has merit. At other times, we may need to do a little reading. For films and video games, we can do that by visiting macro-review sites like RottenTomatoes.com or WhatTheyPlay.com, where we can see multiple reviews from various viewpoints. We should also check out reviews from sources that we know will probably share our worldview and address specific concerns we might have. Talking to friends whose opinions we trust can be helpful, as can reading what cultural commentators and journalists have to say.

The essential point is to get as much information as possible beforehand. And thanks to the Internet, this doesn't usually take much time. Fifteen minutes might be all you need to find the information you're looking for.

If you have a little more time, and you're still not sure if a movie, game, or website is right for a younger audience, check it out for yourself. Watch it, play it, visit it. Search YouTube for trailers or in-game screen captures; download demos; and visit relevant discussion forums. Not only will you have a much more informed opinion on the media in question, but your children (or anyone else who asks you about it) will likely take your opinion much more seriously.

STEP 3: ASK QUESTIONS

When both researching media and using or viewing media, it's important to ask questions about the media and about yourself. To put the key of balance into practice in your home, here are some questions you and your family can ask:

1. Who is the target audience of the media?

2. Is the media appropriate for its target audience?

3. What virtues or vices does the media focus on?

4. What good can viewing or using this media do for me? What harm could viewing or using this media do to me?

5. Does the media depict violence or sexuality? If so, how is that subject matter presented? Why is it presented? In what context does it take place?

6. Do I seek out news and information from a variety of sources on a variety of subjects?

7. How much time do I spend using media for entertainment? For learning? For helping others?

8. How much time do I spend with others, face to face, in relation to how much time I spend using media?

9. How much time do I devote to silent reflection, contemplation, and prayer?

10. Does that division of time reflect what's really important to me?

STEP 4: INTEGRATION

The value of our research and our questioning hinges on our willingness to put what we've learned into practice. With the key of balance, that means we need to:

- Choose to watch movies and television shows or visit websites that will expand our worldview and help us to better understand different cultures and ways of thinking;

- Read a number and variety of political websites to gain a breadth of viewpoints;

- Choose not to watch or use media that puts us in spiritual or physical danger;

- Not unthinkingly reject any form of media without carefully considering its merits;

- Limit the amount of time each day that we use the media purely for our own entertainment;

- Fast, at least occasionally, from media. That fasting can be done regularly—shutting off cell phones at dinnertime, forgoing television on weeknights, or not checking email over the weekend. It can also be done seasonally—giving up non-work and school related Internet use during Lent, staying off social networking sites during Advent, or taking a media-free vacation as a family.

STEP 5: PASSING IT ON

Once we've begun to integrate a balanced approach to media into our own lives, we can help our children learn balance as well. Some ways we can do that include:

- Modeling for them what balanced media use looks like;
- Talking with them about the importance of balance and the dangers of imbalance;
- Asking them to answer the same questions about balance that we ask ourselves;
- Putting reasonable limits on their use of media, i.e. no unlimited texting, no cell phones at the dinner table, no computers in the bedroom, and no more than one hour of television or computer time on school nights;
- Mandating that they spend time alone away from media, reading, journaling, and praying;
- Encouraging them to spend at least one cell phone-free hour a week in Eucharistic adoration.

Again, the ultimate goal of the first media key is to approach media with a worldview that is truly "catholic," that searches "throughout the whole." That's what "catholic" means after all. It comes from the Greek word *katolikos*, a word formed from the words *kata*, meaning "throughout", and *holos*, meaning "the whole."

Looking throughout the whole is our job, yours and mine, not media-makers'. And that's because the key of balance is about us. It's about how we approach and use media. It's about our attitude, about how we think about technology. We are, as Jesus said in Matthew 10:16, to be "wise as serpents," analyzing media from every angle. We're also called to be "innocent as doves," not using media in a way that can harm our minds, our relationships, or our souls.

However, our attitude isn't the only attitude we need to worry about. We also need to worry about the attitude of those making and marketing the media we consume. And that brings us to the second media key: attitude awareness.

Chapter Three

O—π

Attitude Awareness
The Second Media Key

It's called the Ludovico Technique, and in Stanley Kubrick's classic film *Clockwork Orange*, it's what deters the protagonist, Alex DeLarge, from a life of crime.

Strapped to a chair with his eyes pinned open, Alex's doctors force him to watch a series of images depicting graphic and sexually explicit violence. As he stares unblinkingly at the screen, his doctors pump him full of a drug that induces extreme nausea. By the time the Ludovico Treatment concludes, the mere thought of hurting another person makes Alex violently ill.

Clockwork Orange is definitely not family-friendly viewing, so don't necessarily rush out and rent it. But that particular scene illustrates an important truth: what we see affects us. The images we look at and the conditions under which we look at them stay with us. They change us. And on a macro-level, they change our culture.

That's what makes the second media key, attitude awareness, so important. It keeps us on our guard, helping us to maintain a critical perspective about the messages coming at us through the media. It also enables us to be aware of media-makers' agendas, and less susceptible to the subtle yet real brainwashing that can take place when we fail to look at media with a critical eye.

In *Communio et Progressio*, the Church describes the importance of this kind of awareness, writing:

> A training that grounds a man in the basic principles governing the working of the media in human society, as explained above, is nowadays clearly necessary for all. The means of communication genuinely enrich men's minds if their character and function is understood. On the other hand, men who do not sufficiently appreciate their importance, may find their liberty diminished (CP 64).

That's a pretty strong statement. The Church tells us that if we're not aware of the attitudes—the principles, character, and functions—underlying the media we consume, we run the risk of being less free, of being less capable of distinguishing right from wrong and choosing good from bad.

But why is that? What is it that makes us so susceptible?

The Power of the Senses: Understanding Attitude Awareness

We're susceptible to the media's messages because we're sensory creatures. We're spirit and flesh. What comes to us through the flesh—through our eyes, noses, ears, and hands—affects our spirit. And virtually everything we will ever experience comes to us through the flesh.

We acquire knowledge through seeing, hearing, touching, tasting, and smelling. We know we're loved by another when we see love in their eyes, hear it in their voice, and feel it in their touch. We experience friendship in conversation and time spent together, and we experience rejection by the absence of the same. We experience the reality of the world, in all its beauty and tragedy, through our senses.

We also experience salvation through our senses. Since the beginning of time, God has reached us through our bodies. Genesis 2:7 tells us that, "the Lord God formed man of dust from the ground, and breathed into his nostrils the breath of life; and man became a living soul." Only when God touched us, breathed into us His own breath, did man receive life, becoming a "living soul."

And that's still how we receive life. We're cleansed from sin, filled with the Holy Spirit, and given God's own life when God touches us with the waters of Baptism, the oil of Confirmation, and the flesh of Christ in the Eucharist. Likewise, a man's soul becomes a priest's soul through the laying on of hands, and the Sacrament of Marriage is consummated when the bodies of husband and wife become one flesh. Even the very liturgy of the Church reflects this reality. It's filled with sensorial experiences ("smells and bells") that give flesh to sacred realities and speak eternal truths to us in space and time. The Father actually mediates His love to us through the sights, sounds, smells, and movements of the Mass.

There's no getting around it: in God's plan for our redemption, the senses play a powerful part.

But just as our senses can be used to lead us towards God, they also can be used to lead us away from God. Hence the Second Commandment:

> You shall not make for yourself a graven image, or any like-
> ness of anything that is in heaven above, or that is in the earth
> beneath, or that is in the water under the earth; you shall not
> bow down to them or serve them (Ex. 20:4–5).

That commandment is there because human beings are a sensory people, a media people you could almost say. We're drawn to what we can see, taste, hear, and touch. We're drawn to the visible. And we're inclined to worship it, to care more about it than what we can't see, hear, taste, and touch.

That tendency got our spiritual ancestors, the Israelites, into big trouble several thousand years ago when they opted to worship a golden calf rather than the invisible God who led them out of Egypt. And it still gets us into trouble when we choose to place our trust in the things of the world and not in Christ. It also gets us into trouble when we give more credence to media's messages than we do to natural and divine law.

The power of media lies in its appeal to our senses. The second media key, attitude awareness, reminds us of the power of that appeal, an appeal that enables media not just to reflect reality, but also, in the words of the Pontifical Council for Social Communications, to be "a mirror that helps shape the reality it reflects." *

The second media key likewise reminds us that there is an attitude behind all media. It urges us not to forget that every advertiser, every producer, every writer, and every software designer has an agenda. They have a point of view, a purpose, a goal. And because of that, every piece of media carries some kind of message. It's been created and designed to convey the point of view of the media-maker and to achieve the goal they set out for their creation. This is true regardless of whether the media-maker is fully aware of that goal or not.

Finally, when applied, the second media key helps us cultivate an awareness of the attitudes underlying the media we view and use. It enables us to more clearly recognize the messages, both subtle and not so subtle, coming at us through media, so that we don't allow visible lies to override invisible truths.

---

* Pontifical Council for Social Communications, *Ethics in Advertising* (February 22, 1997), 3. Available at www.vatican.va/roman_curia/pontifical_councils/pccs. (hereafter cited in text as EA)

Seeing Clearly: Illustrating Attitude Awareness

WITH ONE EYE OPEN

Sometimes an awareness of the attitudes underlying media comes easily. It doesn't take much work on our part to understand the message being presented because the media-makers have already done the work for us, putting their message front and center in the media's marketing campaign.

For example, the 2009 bio-epic *Milk*, which celebrated the life of homosexual activist Harvey Milk, made no bones about its underlying premise: homosexuality is natural, laws against it are wrong, and Harvey Milk was the gay messiah. That premise was boldly announced in the movie's tagline: "His life changed history. His courage changed lives." It was also demonstrated in the film's trailer. With a stirring operatic score playing in the background—a score which featured chorus after chorus of "Alleluias"—the trailer shows Milk defying death threats to speak to crowds of homosexual activists, calling out for equal rights as he stands on the steps of the Capitol, and riding on a float in a parade with confetti flying behind him. No less than ten sequences in the two-minute trailer feature cheering crowds. Another ten feature Milk's persecution at the hands of city and state officials.

You don't need to be a deeply perceptive person to recognize the attitude underlying *Milk*. You don't even need to watch the movie to see this attitude in action. The trailer gives you all you need.

The same goes for many websites, where the prevailing attitude is made obvious in the site's mission statement or tagline. The Daily Kos defines itself as a "Daily Weblog with political analysis on U.S. current events from a liberal perspective," and proudly announces that its contributors include Barack Obama, Nancy Pelosi, and Jimmy Carter. On the other side of the spectrum, National Review's "The Corner" describes itself as a "multi-author conservative Weblog."

In those cases, the perspective of the media is stated clearly for all to see. As long as we keep one eye open, we can know from the very start what we're getting ourselves into. More often, however, media's messages are far more nuanced.

BOTH EYES REQUIRED

Commercials are an obvious example of this. On the surface, the message of a television commercial may seem straightforward enough. It's selling something—a gadget, a beauty product, a luxury automobile. But underneath that obvious sales pitch, there's usually another attitude at work. In order to sell their products, the Pontifical Council for Social Communications points out, advertisers "are selective about the values and attitudes to be fostered and encouraged, promoting some while ignoring others."

In the case of most commercials, the overriding attitude they promote, the Council continues, is that "an abundance of possessions leads to happiness and fulfillment" (EA 3).

Case in point: Pantene commercials featuring beautiful actresses with lustrous locks or Mazda commercials featuring ruggedly handsome men and their blonde, curvaceous girlfriends. Neither commercial simply sells a lifestyle. They make a promise: if you buy this product, you too will be beautiful; you too will have a sexy girlfriend; you too will be happy.

Similarly subtle but deadly messages are woven into seemingly innocuous videogames like *The Sims* (and its sequels). On the surface, *The Sims* is about developing life skills, about building a life and building it well. The overt sexuality and criminality prevalent in so many other games is absent, which is a good thing. But the problem with *The Sims* (and other games like it) is what the creators consider a well-built life.

In these games, players design their own characters from a list of given traits and progress in the game by acquiring more "stuff"—houses, cars, electronics—as well as by becoming more popular or successful. The idea that a good life consists of more possessions is bad enough, but worse still is that none of the personality traits players can select for their avatars include the virtues necessary for living a truly good life. Try as you might, you can't construct an avatar that is temperate, patient, charitable, faithful, prudent, or just. In the world of *The Sims* (and most other games), those virtues are virtually non-existent. If we're not keeping both eyes open, it's easy to miss that message and, unwittingly, buy into the attitude of the media's makers.

It's equally easy to miss the hidden agendas and messages woven into movies and television shows. Subtly dangerous attitudes are nearly everywhere media is, from prime time dramas—where the desire to "normalize" homosexuality has led to nearly every hit show featuring at least one homosexual character (so often depicted as the sensitive, sympathetic best friend)—to romantic comedies—where the idea that love is about sex, not marriage, means the hero and heroine must sleep together before the film's end.

I say "nearly everywhere" because, of course, not all attitudes coming to us through the media, up front or otherwise, are negative. The attitudes behind many forms of media conform to a Catholic vision of the good, the true, and the beautiful.

That's the case for media that aims to promote greater understanding of the Catholic Faith, such as websites like CUF.org, television networks like EWTN, and radio networks like Relevant Radio. That also can be the case with films or television shows that aim to give people deeper insight into questions of social justice or human dignity. Movies such as *Guess Who's Coming to Dinner*, which challenged racial prejudice among America's middle class, or *Life is Beautiful*, which celebrated the love between a husband and wife and the sacrificial nature of fatherhood, were shaped by an attitude that was in line with a Catholic vision of truth. Their creators still had an agenda—it just happened to be a good agenda.

The second media key is really as much about recognizing the positive attitudes underlying media as it is about recognizing the negative attitudes. It's about opening our eyes to all the messages the media sends our way—good and bad. It's just that the stakes for failing to recognize the bad are considerably higher.

Preserving True Freedom:
Why Attitude Awareness Matters

When we fail to recognize the good in media, we might miss out on a beautiful story or an important piece of news or information. But we don't generally put ourselves in spiritual danger. The same doesn't hold true when we fail to recognize damaging or dangerous attitudes.

Again, what we experience through the media affects us. Recall those statistics mentioned in Chapter One of this book. From the 2004 Rand Institute study—which concluded that teens who watch shows with a high amount of sexual content are twice as likely to be sexually active—to the 2002 Columbia University study—which found a 60 percent increase of violent behaviors in adults who watched large amounts of violence on film as children—the consensus is almost unilateral. Watching sex and violence can contribute to sexual and violent thoughts and lead to sexual and violent behavior. [23]

If what we see can affect how we act, it most certainly can affect how we think. It can affect the choices we make. It can lead us to believe that we will be happier if we buy the products that advertisers peddle. It can encourage us to buy into the idea that success is about possessions. And it can start to subtly twist our understanding of right and wrong.

Consider these numbers from Gallup:

In 1983, only 34 percent of Americans believed homosexuality was an acceptable practice. By 2009, that number had risen to 54 percent (and to

62 percent among 18–29 year olds). Similarly, in 1969, only 21 percent of Americans believed that sex outside of marriage was morally legitimate. By 2009, that climbed to 62 percent.[24]

Unfortunately, the picture grows even grimmer with non-Catholics removed from the mix. A 2009 Gallup poll concluded that more Catholics approve of sex outside of marriage than non-Catholics (67 percent versus 57 percent). They also approve more widely of homosexuality (again by a whopping 10 percentage points) and divorce (by a margin of 5 percentage points).[25]

Obviously, the inclusion of a homosexual character on *House* can't alone bear the blame for statistics like that. Multiple factors are at work. But media's attitude towards sexuality can't be entirely discounted. For well over a decade, network news has regularly cast the push for gay rights and same-sex "marriage" as a civil rights issue. Likewise, both homosexuality and pre-marital sex have become commonplace in prime time, and not just in adult programming. The teen hits *Glee*, *Gossip Girl*, and the new *Beverly Hills 90210* (just to name a few) prominently and proudly feature homosexual characters and sexually active teenagers. On a nightly basis, Americans of all ages watch—and increasingly accept as normal—behavior once considered gravely wrong. And that watching has its effect, even on people who should know better. Again, as the Church said in 1997, the media "is a mirror that helps shape the reality it reflects."

Even those of us who still subscribe to the Church's teachings on homosexuality and premarital sex can't entirely discount the media's affect on us. The victories of those who promote a damaging agenda can be just as subtle as their messages. They achieve victory, at least to some degree, every time we smile when our favorite couple "finally" sleeps together on a TV show. They also achieve victory when we find ourselves tuning in to re-runs of *Will and Grace* or silently cheering because the protagonist in a film has shot the villain and got his much desired revenge. That's what media can do. It can arouse feelings in us that directly contradict what we believe to be true and right.

What's true in entertainment is equally true in politics.

From false newspaper stories in England heralding the nobility of the suicidal Charge of the Light Brigade during the Crimean War to American posters of the German "Hun" devouring women and children during World War I, media propaganda has long been a staple of raising support for government war efforts. Media propaganda has likewise encouraged support for peacetime policies in countless countries, including Soviet Russia and Communist China, where stories, films, and posters promoted the goodness of the workers, the glory of the collective, and the evils of capitalism. It was used even more effectively in Hitler's Germany, where propaganda films such as *The Eternal Jew*—which contrasted images of rats scurrying out of sewers to Jews living in squalor—helped move otherwise decent people to perpetrate horrific acts of racial brutality.

That's the potential power of media. It's a power of which the Church is aware, and it's a power that she has strongly cautioned us against, writing:

> "It can never be forgotten that communication through the media is not a utilitarian exercise intended simply to motivate, persuade or sell. Still less is it a vehicle for ideology. The media can at times reduce human beings to units of consumption or competing interest groups, or manipulate viewers and readers and listeners as mere ciphers from whom some advantage is sought, whether product sales or political support; and these things destroy community. It is the task of communication to bring people together and enrich their lives, not isolate and exploit them."[26]

Much depends on media-makers. They wield an incredibly powerful tool. But much also depends on us. We can't control what messages media-makers send out. But we can control our awareness of those messages. We can be more than passive consumers, blindly taking in whatever ideology filmmakers or game designers put forth. We can be, and we should be. Our freedom depends upon it.

Applying the Second Media Key

STEP 1: PRAY
Pray for the cardinal virtue of prudence.

According to the *Catechism of the Catholic Church*, "Prudence is the virtue that disposes practical reason to discern our true good in every circumstance and to choose the right means of achieving it...it guides the other virtues by setting rule and measure. It is prudence that immediately guides the judgment of conscience. The prudent man determines and directs his conduct in accordance with this judgment. With the help of this virtue we apply moral principles to particular cases without error and overcome doubts about the good to achieve and the evil to avoid" (CCC 1806).

STEP 2: RESEARCH
Like the first media key, applying the second media key requires research.

If it's a film or game, start again by reading reviews. And read those reviews not just for critics' thoughts about the acting or cinematography, but also for the overall message of the film.

Look for commentary on the film's message or target audience. Interviews with actors, directors, screenwriters, or game creators also can shed light on the media's underlying agenda.

Simply viewing the movie's trailer can do the same. For film and television, all of these tools can be found easily by visiting the Internet Movie Database (imdb.com). The "extras" included on most DVDs can likewise help us make sense of what we're seeing.

For websites or Internet-based tools, always look for a mission statement or an "About" category on the menu bar. Also, find out who the contributors are to a Web-based magazine or blog, and look to see if their cultural or political perspective is designated.

STEP 3: ASK QUESTIONS

1. Who is the hero or heroine and what virtues or vices characterize them?

2. What major decisions does the hero or heroine make? What are the consequences of those decisions?

3. Do the characters abide by any moral norms? Are the characters rewarded for abiding by moral norms or are they rewarded for not abiding by them?

4. Who is portrayed in a positive light? Who is portrayed in a negative light? Who is the enemy and what characterizes them?

5. What is the media's attitude towards God and people of faith or virtue?

6. What does the media present as desirable? How do the language, imagery, or sounds reinforce the media's message?

7. Who is producing or making this media? What is their worldview or agenda?

8. How is the media attempting to affect me? What does it want me to believe?

9. How is the media affecting me? In what ways am I reacting sympathetically to it? Is that sympathy in any way in conflict with my core values?

10. Has the media in any way changed how I think about something? Has that change moved me closer to God's way of thinking or farther away from it?

STEP 4: INTEGRATION

☛ Talk about the film, game, or website with others after using it or viewing it and discuss its overall theme.

☞ Get news from multiple sources in order to pinpoint the different agendas of news providers.

☞ When viewing commercials, question the attitudes and value systems underlying them. Watch them with an eye to the ideals and lifestyle they promote.

☞ Practice the occasional media fast, recommended by the key of balance, in order to gain perspective on the media and recognize the claims of products and technologies for the marketing ploys that most of them are.

STEP 5: PASSING IT ON

☞ Use or view media with children the first time they view it or use it. That means sitting down and watching the show, looking at a website, or playing a video game with them—even though this can feel like penance. Remember, you can always "offer it up."

☞ Talk with children about the media you've just watched or used together, asking them the same questions you ask yourself and pointing out to them where the characters succeed or fail according to a Catholic worldview.

☞ During commercial breaks, ask them to identify the values different advertisements are promoting.

☞ Explain the difference between websites and talk with them about why different websites have been created (i.e. to promote an institution, a product, a way of thinking, or to meet a specific set of interests of a particular audience).

☞ Ask them to identify what they think is fact and what they think is opinion on blogs or in essays, and quiz them on what political or ideological perspective different writers or journals seem to have based on their writing.

As media consumers we're not brainless automatons, controlled by whatever messages media sends. But we are affected by media. How we view relationships, politics, faith, meaning, and any number of realities can be influenced by what we see. We're visual people, media people, with an inherited tendency to worship the visible.

For good and for ill, people will try to take advantage of that tendency. They will attempt to use media to tell us what to think and what to do, as well as how we should see ourselves, the universe, and all it contains. The second media key—attitude awareness—works to loosen the media's hold on us. When used, it makes us less susceptible to emotional and intellectual manipulation. It also lays the groundwork for the next media key: the dignity of the human person.

Chapter Four

O━┓

The Dignity of the Human Person
The Third Media Key

It's an old film and hard to find. Netflix has it, but most video stores don't. Add to the mix the English subtitles, which render the Japanese dialogue understandable, and the fact that the director chose to shoot the film in black and white, and it can be tempting to dismiss the film as too artsy or highbrow for regular viewers.

But that would be a mistake.

Released in 1956, *The Burmese Harp* tells the tale of a group of Japanese soldiers captured in Burma at the end of World War II. One soldier, Mizushima, separated from his platoon, makes his way across the countryside alone. And as he walks, the horror of war comes home to him through the bodies of his fallen comrades. Thousands of them lie along his path, rotting in both sun and shade. Before rejoining his comrades, who are about to be shipped home to Japan, Mizushima makes a decision: he will not return home until he has buried every Japanese bone and body left in Burma. He will dedicate his life to honoring the fallen, and he will honor them by honoring their bodies.

For good reason, *The Burmese Harp* is on the Vatican's list of 45 "important" films.* The lesson it teaches exemplifies what John Paul II described as the goal of all technological progress: man becoming more human.

In his encyclical *Redemptor Hominis,* the pope asks:

> Does this [technological] progress, which has man for its author and promoter, make human life on earth "more human" in every aspect of that life? Does it make it more "worthy of man"? There can be no doubt that in various aspects it does. But the question keeps coming back with regard to what is most essential—whether in the context of this progress man, as man, is becoming truly better, that is to say more mature spiritually, more aware of the dignity of his humanity, more responsible, more open to others, especially the neediest and the weakest, and readier to give and to aid all.[†]

Making man "more worthy of man"—that's the third media key. All media should reflect, uphold, and enhance human dignity. It should, like that Japanese soldier in *The Burmese Harp,* reverence the human body and the human spirit. It should bring people together. It should promote understanding of the human person and human communities. And it should shed light on what makes the human person unique in all creation.

---

[*] "Other films from other cultural environments relate to a different order of values which nevertheless have certain important affinities with Christian culture, such as, for example, those which derive from the spiritual resources of the ancient civilizations of the Orient...[Some such films], rich with intimistic sensibilities which to Christians reveal the features of those virtues defined by the Fathers of the Church, when they found them expressed in the works of pagan writers, as *naturaliter cristianae.* Their films are not restricted to addressing the question of values in a veiled and restrained manner for educational or propagandistic purposes but each time invent new ways of approaching a reality outwardly manifested in signs and tokens which, when correctly interpreted, lead to the discovery of an interior world rich with spirituality" (Pontifical Council for Social Communications, 100 Years of Cinema, January 1, 1996, no. 13); "Vatican Best Films List" is available at http://www.nccbuscc.org/fb/vaticanfilms.htm.

[†] John Paul II, Encyclical Letter *Redemptoris Hominis* (March 4, 1979), 15. Available at http://www.vatican.va/holy_father/john_paul_ii (hereafter cited in text as RH).

In God's Image: Understanding the Third Media Key

The origins of the third media key go all the way back to the Garden. In Eden, after creating the heavens and the earth, the sea and the sky, the fish, the birds, and all the other animals, God pronounced His work "good." But when He finished creating man, He pronounced His work "very good" (Gen. 1:31). Nothing else in the universe got a "very good" from God. From the beginning, the human person was set apart. And that, we're told in Genesis 1:26, is because the human person was created in the image and likeness of God.

Obviously, that doesn't mean that we inherited God's nose or eyes. Rather, we resemble Him in spirit. Unlike the animals, we have a soul, a capacity to give ourselves in love and choose good or evil. We have free will.

We also have a body. Or, more accurately, we are a body. The human person is equal parts matter and spirit, flesh and soul. Our bodies aren't cages that contain a soul. They're part of us, and because of that, they too have a great dignity. St. Paul tells us as much when he writes in 1 Corinthians 6:19–20, "Do you not know that your body is a temple of the Holy Spirit within you, which you have from God? You are not your own; you were bought with a price. So glorify God in your body."

St. Paul also makes it clear that this great dignity we possess belongs to every member of the human community. "There is neither Jew nor Greek, there is neither slave nor free, there is neither male nor female; for you are all one in Christ Jesus" (Gal. 3:28).

These are the truths by which man is to live. In life, we're supposed to nurture our spirits, care for our bodies, give ourselves in love, and defend the dignity of others. And nothing changes, or at least nothing should change, in the realm of media.

Media should help us understand our dignity and the dignity of others. Media should also help us understand the importance of giving ourselves in love to others. It should take into consideration all that we are—body and soul, heart and mind—and both reflect and defend that. Films, television shows, and video games should illuminate those truths, while social media, such as the Internet and cell phones, should help us realize those truths—they should help us actualize them.

And when they don't, when they fail in any of those regards, they fail as media.

Media doesn't exist in a vacuum. It's a tool that exists to serve the human person, to serve the entire human community. If it's not doing that, it's not meeting the standards that God has set for media. It's not doing what media is supposed to do. It is, quite simply, not good media.

The same truth applies to us. When we use media in a way that doesn't reflect, uphold, and defend our dignity or the dignity of others, and when we use media to isolate others or ourselves from the human community, we're also being less than what we're supposed to be. We're acting less than fully human. We're not making ourselves "more worthy of man," but rather less worthy.

The Pontifical Council for Social Communications summed up that relationship in *Ethics in Communication*, noting that, "The human person and the human community are the end and measure of the use of the media of social communication; communication should be by persons to persons for the integral development of persons."[‡]

[‡] Pontifical Council for Social Communication, *Ethics in Communication* (June 2, 2000), 21. Available at www.vatican.va/roman_curia/pontifical_councils/pccs (hereafter cited in text as EC).

The Measure and the End:
Illustrating the Third Media Key

RECOGNIZING RESPECT (AND DISRESPECT) FOR HUMAN DIGNITY ON FILM

An innate understanding of the Pontifical Council's admonition—that the human person should be the "end and measure of the media"—is what makes *The Burmese Harp* so great. The reverence Mizushima has for the bodies of his fallen comrades and the intense brotherhood among the Japanese soldiers show us what is both required and possible for our fallen human race. Reverence for the human person is the substantive message of the film and the end it attempts to further.

Similarly, the movie *Bella*, which recounts one man's determination to prevent a female friend from aborting her unborn child, reflects the Council's words by offering a moving testimony to the dignity that even the smallest and weakest members of the human race possess. It uses drama and story to make an argument that has been made over and over again in the political and moral sphere, and it is all the more powerful for that.

From classic films like *Going My Way* to modern movies such as *Phoebe in Wonderland* and *I Am Sam*, the dramatic arts can help us better recognize the dignity of the elderly, children, and individuals with special needs. They show us what we might not encounter, or be willing to encounter, in the real world. They give us a glimpse into the lives of those not like our families or ourselves. And they teach us that despite differences in age or ability, much still connects us.

Unfortunately, for every good example of media defending human dignity, there seem to be ten examples of media undermining human dignity. As with the key of attitude awareness, some of those examples are glaringly obvious—and none more so than pornography.

Pornography reduces human beings to the level of animals, controlled by appetites and motivated by little more than a selfish desire for pleasure. Absent is all that makes man the image and likeness of God—reverence for body and soul, a willingness to give and sacrifice for others, and the ability to control, restrain, and properly direct one's desires.

The same can be said of slasher or torture porn films. From *Halloween* to *Saw,* reverence for the body is as absent from these films as an understanding of the role of free will and human choice in evil. The films reduce humans to pieces of meat, with one life after another "sacrificed" to a thirst for blood, a thirst viewed by many as "entertainment."

Those are the obvious examples. But Hollywood has also found much more subtle ways to undermine the dignity of the human person, from movies that promote assisted-suicide and abortion (e.g. *Million Dollar Baby, Dirty Dancing,* and *Cider House Rules*) to action flicks whose body count by movie's end exceeds the total population of some small cities (e.g. *Kill Bill, Wanted,* or *Natural Born Killers).* Even reality television has taken a swing at human dignity. When the failings and quirks of actual people are used as grist for viewer entertainment, persons—who are supposed to be treated as subjects—are turned into objects. And that's never a transformation that reflects the dignity of the human person.

PRACTICING RESPECT FOR THE DIGNITY OF THE HUMAN PERSON WITH SOCIAL MEDIA

In its document, *Ethics in Internet*, the Pontifical Council for Social Communications acknowledges that, "When based upon shared values rooted in the nature of the person, the intercultural dialogue made possible by the Internet and other media of social communication can be 'a privileged means for building the civilization of love'" (EI 9).

In other words, social media can bring people together and help us create a world that is more truly human, a civilization governed by charity.

Where film can illuminate the dignity of the human person, social media can help us actualize our dignity. It can help us live it and express it.

Connected via social networking sites, Internet chat rooms, discussion forums, and more, we can encounter people from different countries and cultures, learning from each other and forming friendships with those who share our faith, interests, and passions. If we're single, online dating sites like Catholic Match and Ave Maria Singles can help us find the person God intends for us to marry. Similarly, if we're struggling with doubts about our faith, intellectual questions, or the effects of addiction and abuse, we can find help online. We can also be the ones offering help online, giving guidance and counsel to those in need. We can put our knowledge, wisdom, and experience at the service of others via the Internet. Every day, in countless ways, social media gives us the opportunity to conform our lives to God's plan and become more fully human.

But that only happens when we use social media wisely—when we use it to facilitate, not replace, real world relationships, and when we use it to enrich our lives, not avoid our lives. When we don't use it wisely, we can participate in stripping others and ourselves of our God-given dignity.

That's true of anyone who has ever used the Internet to spread gossip or lies. Increasingly common among young people, "cyber-bullying" has already resulted in multiple suicides, and many colleges and universities have banned students from participating in gossip forums such as "Juicy Campus," due to the emotional trauma suffered by the students singled out on the sites.[27]

It's also true of anyone who uses social media for selfish ends—glorifying themselves and garnering attention by posting inappropriate pictures on MySpace, broadcasting details of relationships on Facebook, and sending out their every thought and action via Twitter.

In his book, *Fame Junkies*, author Jake Halpern links those habits with a marked increase in narcissism—an overweening vanity and self-absorption—and cites studies by Keith Campbell at the University of Georgia that indicate that on the Narcissism Personality Index, no other demographic group in any other part of the world scores as high as the American teenager.[28]

Halpern is just one of many voices raising concerns about social media encouraging selfishness and self-absorption. A slew of articles, from *The Weekly Standard* to *The Chronicle of Higher Education*, have also commented on the link. In one of those articles, a vice president of a Catholic university succinctly summed up the situation, saying:

> "Having your own Web page, creating a virtual persona—and a shallow one at that—gives everyone a stage on which to perform. Behaviors that would have been unthinkable a decade ago are now perfectly acceptable. Culturally, I think we're setting ourselves up for an epidemic of narcissism."[29]

Even more problematic than abuses of Facebook, however, are abuses of virtual communities like Second Life, an online virtual world where people have the opportunity to design for themselves the life they've always wanted.

There's good to be found in Second Life, like the chance to explore a 3-D "re-creation" of Camelot or watch all thirty-eight of William Shakespeare's plays performed by virtual actors. But evidenced by stories such as this one from MSNBC, there's also much that's deeply problematic.

> Max, 39, isn't sure what drove his soon-to-be-ex-wife to have a relationship in Second Life. He says she refused to talk about it, and if he asked questions, she'd just hop online and freeze him out.

> "I thought she was going through a depression and she'd get bored and move on with life," he says. "But she kept getting deeper and deeper."

Within six months of signing up for Second Life, Max's wife was spending up to eight hours a day online—and even more on the weekends. She and her in-world boyfriend were in constant contact—even when they weren't in-world.

Max says he found out later that his wife and her avatar boyfriend were having drinks together—in his house—via Web cam. Max went on Google and started doing some detective work. To his amazement, he learned that his wife had married her in-world boyfriend in Second Life.[30]

That's an extreme example. Most people involved in virtual communities won't "marry" someone online, but any of us who have spent too much time commenting on blog posts or updating our "status" on Facebook can be guilty of the same neglect of human relationships in the real world. So can those of us who have confused the true meaning of friendship—a relationship that entails commitment and a readiness to sacrifice for another—with a number, a list of names on our Facebook page that includes hundreds or even thousands of people whom we barely know.

Likewise, trying to maintain a relationship with that list of names can inevitably do little but distract us from maintaining the relationships that really do matter. Only God can fully love and know billions of souls. The rest of us have a more limited capacity. And that capacity is generally far lower than even the most conservative number of "Facebook Friends."

For teens, who have never known anything but social networking via computer and cell phone, the dangers to interpersonal communication are even more acute.

In 2009, articles in both secular sources such as *USA Today* and Catholic sources such as *Our Sunday Visitor* reported anecdotal evidence that suggests all that text-messaging, not to mention Facebook posting and instant messaging, is changing the way teens communicate and understand friendship.[31]

In the *Our Sunday Visitor* story, one high school teacher said of his students, "They communicate more frequently, but less personally. They struggle to express what's important to them and to organize their thoughts because they've grown accustomed to having conversations one line at a time."

That same story chronicled the struggle of Rebecca Arnold, a Catholic mother of five, who told *Our Sunday Visitor* about how her two oldest daughters—ages twenty-three and fourteen—both prefer texting or instant messaging their friends to actually talking with them.

"Phone calls last five minutes at the most," she said in the article. "I'd be happy to get Kathleen [her fourteen-year-old daughter] a phone for her room, but at this point, she doesn't want one."

The reason?

According to her daughter, "I don't know what my friends and I would talk about."

Unfortunately, young adults' communications skills aren't proving much better than their teenage counterparts. A 2005 report found that 34 percent of employers were dissatisfied with the oral communication skills of high school graduates. Similar studies conclude that employers are increasingly dissatisfied with young employees' writing skills.[32]

Add to the mix those who view online pornography, those who engage in "sexting," and those who let cell phone conversations and text messages pull their attention away from the people they're with, and it's easy to see why the Church, for all the good social media can do, has said:

> "Paradoxically, the very forces which can lead to better communication can also lead to increasing self-centeredness and alienation." The Internet can unite people, but it also can divide them, both as individuals and as mutually suspicious groups separated by ideology, politics, possessions, race

and ethnicity, intergenerational differences, and even religion (EI 9).

Illuminating and Obscuring: Why the Third Media Key Matters

When we watch movies or television shows that create a false image of the human person, that's a problem. When we neglect both charity and humility in our use of the media, that's a problem. When virtual relationships become more important than real world relationships, that's also a problem. And when we invest time, energy, and money in creating the life we've always wanted for ourselves online, instead of investing time, energy, and money in bringing our real life into conformity with God's plan, that is a serious problem.

Each and every one of those choices leads us away from the human community and away from the world of bodies, with all their flaws and limitations, but also with all their beauty. That's why it's critical that both the media we view and the media we use reflect the dignity of the human person.

As the discussion of the second media key, attitude awareness, made clear, human beings are sensory creatures. What we think and feel is profoundly affected by what we see and hear. Accordingly, Pope Paul VI in *Inter Mirifica* tells us that audio-visual media can, in a particularly powerful way, "bring about a deeper knowledge and study of humanity and, with the aid of appropriately heightened dramatic effects, can reveal and glorify the grand dimensions of truth and goodness" (IM 7).

That's what makes films such as *The Burmese Harp* or *Bella* so powerful. The heightened power of dramatic storytelling illuminates truths about the human person that we might miss in the day-to-day world.

But the opposite is also true. Just as audio-visual media can "reveal and glorify the grand dimensions of truth and goodness," it can also obscure them. It can use drama, music, lighting, scenery, costumes, and artfully crafted dialogue to paint a false picture of man. It can reduce him to a body or reduce him to a soul. It can obscure the importance of free will, and create an image of man controlled entirely by circumstance or biological impulse. It can confuse us about the dignity of human life.

When it comes to the media we use, the positive and negative consequences are even more pronounced. We might watch a movie that glorifies the human person and walk away only minimally affected. But our life changes when we make a new friend or connect with an old friend via social networking sites. Our life changes when we meet the person we're going to marry via a Catholic dating site. Our life changes when we come to understand and respect another's culture or beliefs through reading about it online.

Our life also changes when we start neglecting our spouse for Facebook, when we spend hours each day on websites like Second Life, or when we forget how important it is to look in the eyes of the person we're speaking with, instead of repeatedly checking our email on our iPhones.

No matter what, our use of social media does change us. And we're the ones who determine whether it changes us for better or for worse.

Applying the Third Media Key

STEP 1: PRAY
Pray for the cardinal virtue of justice.

The *Catechism of the Catholic Church* explains, "Justice is the moral virtue that consists in the constant and firm will to give their due to God and neighbor. Justice toward God is called the 'virtue of religion.' Justice toward men disposes one to respect the rights of each and to establish in human relationships the harmony that promotes equity with regard to persons and to the common good. The just man, often mentioned in the Sacred Scriptures, is distinguished by habitual right thinking and the uprightness of his conduct toward his neighbor" (CCC 1807).

STEP 2: RESEARCH

This step never changes. *Read* up on films, television shows, and video games. *Look* for cultural commentary on social media tools. *Talk* to people you trust. *Gather* as much information as you can beforehand, so that as often as possible you don't use or view any media without at least a rough idea of what it has to say about (or how it can affect) the human person.

STEP 3: ASK QUESTIONS

1. Are the characters in a film or television show depicted as being responsible for their own choices? How?
2. Is the human body treated with respect in this media? If so, how? If not, why? Is the gift of life taken seriously, or are lives casually and callously snuffed out?
3. How does the media depict children, the elderly, or individuals with special needs? Are any people treated with less dignity than others?
4. In what ways do the characters give of themselves to others? What motivates that gift?
5. How much time do I spend communicating with others online? How does that compare with the time I spend with people face-to-face?
6. Am I neglecting any of my responsibilities—school, work, prayer, family, friends, finances, service, or prayer—in order to spend time online or play video games? If so, why?

7. How often do I interrupt a conversation with friends to take a phone call, check email, or "Twitter" a thought? How often, when in a group of people, do I tune out and use a mobile device to communicate with people who aren't in the room?

8. How many of my activities online lead to real world interactions or help facilitate activities in the real world?

9. If I use a social networking site or Twitter, what is my motivation behind the things I post and messages I tweet? Am I seeking attention? Am I trying to improve others' opinions of me? Am I maintaining appropriate boundaries? Why do I think it's important to post or tweet what I do?

10. How does the media I use and view affect others? Have I ever used media to hurt someone's feelings or reputation? Have I ever treated others like objects in my use of the media?

STEP 4: INTEGRATION

☞ Avoid films, television shows, or video games that ultimately paint a false picture of the human person.

☞ Refuse to view pornography, as well as reality TV shows based on the premise that real people should be objects for entertainment.

☞ Recommend and commend films, shows, and video games that highlight the beauty and dignity of the human person.

☞ If you're spending time with another person or a group of people, only answer the cell phone or respond to text messages when it's absolutely necessary.

☞ Don't say "yes" to every "Friend Request" on Facebook. While it's a pity that the online social networking term for not accepting a person's "Friend Request" is to choose to "ignore" the person, it just isn't necessarily prudent to say "yes" to every "Friend Request." In general, it's best to use social networking sites primarily for keeping in touch with the people you really care about.

☞ Don't post intimate details about relationships or family situations on social networking sites.

☞ Never use technology to spread gossip or speak ill of others.

☞ Limit time spent in virtual communities such as Second Life, and only use them if they facilitate real world relationships and learning.

☞ Listen to friends or family members if they say you're spending too much time online/on your cell phone/playing video games, and then change your behavior.

STEP 5: PASSING IT ON

☞ When possible, don't permit young children or students to view media that undermines human dignity. Talk to them about your decision, and give them specific reasons why that media paints a false picture of the human person.

☞ Watch movies and play games with your child. Afterwards, talk about what the movie has to say about the human person.

☞ If you choose to permit your children to participate in a social networking site, it is both loving and prudent to have them give you access to the site. If you observe something there that seems amiss, talk with them about it.

☞ Don't allow your child to send or receive text messages during meal times or when you're doing something together as a family.

☞ Encourage them to call their friends rather than texting, instant messaging, or emailing them.

☞ Open up your home so they can invite friends over and meet them in person.

☞ Keep the computer in a public space in the home, and limit the time that can be spent on it each night.

☞ Ban the use of iPods and headphones in the car. Engage the whole family in conversation as much as possible, or listen to

music or books on tape together when you drive, then talk about
what you've just heard.

O—™

Of all the psalms in the Bible, Psalm 8 might come closest to expressing
man's wonder at his own dignity. It asks:

> What is man that thou art mindful of him,
> and the son of man that thou dost care for him?
> Yet thou hast made him little less than God,
> and dost crown him with glory and honor.
> Thou hast given him dominion over the works of thy hands;
> thou hast put all things under his feet...
>
> Psalms 8:4–6

As long as we live, that is a question we should never cease to ask and a
truth we should never cease to marvel at. Each and every person, by the
mere fact of our creation, has been made just a little less than God. Next
to his saving love, our own dignity is the central truth of our lives, a truth
intended to guide us in all our thoughts and actions and a truth to be
preached through all our words and deeds. That's true in the real world,
and that's true in the digital world.

But in both worlds, our dignity is not the only truth that matters. Truth
itself matters.

Chapter Five

O⸺

Truth-Filled

The Fourth Media Key

Ever dreamed of becoming a vampire? Or maybe a ninja? What about a marauding cyberpunk? A tiger? Even just a plain old leggy blonde with the perfect tan? Whatever identity you've secretly longed to assume, your dream can become a (virtual) reality in the online virtual world of Second Life. There, the rules of nature need not apply. Your true self, with all its inherent limitations, can be hidden and left behind.

Taking your place in Second Life will be an avatar—the virtual persona who moves in response to your commands through the online world. Via your avatar, you can be whoever you want to be, do whatever you want to do, look however you want to look. And you can be that way for as long as you like—a week, a month, a year. In Second Life, you can try on a new persona like you try on clothes: see what fits, walk around in it for a while, then cast it off if it doesn't suit.

That ability is one of the main attractions of Second Life.

In the flash video welcoming users to the site, its creators urge people to, "Be yourself. Free yourself. Love your look. Love your life." They also promise that, "The only limit is your imagination."

For many, it's a tempting promise. But it's also a false promise. No lie can ever set you free. Only the truth can do that.

That was Christ's promise in John 8:32: "You will know the truth, and the truth will make you free." That's also a promise media can help fulfill. Media, properly crafted and used, can be a tool for conveying truth— truth about God, truth about the human person, and truth about each one of us. That's the fourth media key: truth-filled. This key tells us that the media we watch, listen to, read, and play should be filled with truth. It should not tell lies about God or about the human condition.

It also tells us that we should not tell lies either. When we use media, when we enter online communities and virtual worlds, we mustn't leave the truth behind. In word and action, our use of media should be filled with truth. It should conform to reality and help lead others to a deeper understanding of reality.

Communio et Progressio sums up the fourth media key when it states:

> Every communication must comply with certain essential re-
> quirements and these are sincerity, honesty and truthfulness.
> Good intentions and a clear conscience do not thereby make
> a communication sound and reliable. A communication must
> state the truth (CP 17).

That, of course, begs the question: what is truth?

Quid est Veritas?
Understanding the Fourth Media Key

THE FUNDAMENTALS OF TRUTH
Two thousand years ago, Pontius Pilate looked Christ in the eye and asked, *"Quid est veritas?"* Today, that's the question of an entire culture. What is truth? Does it exist? And if it does, how are we to know it?

We live in a post-modern world, a world defined by intellectual and moral agnosticism. As a whole, the culture shies away from absolutes. It prefers seeking to finding, and asking to answering. Tolerance and the withholding of judgment are perhaps the only actions considered absolute moral goods. Everything else is relative. It's up to individuals to determine right from wrong, good from bad, true from false.

That's a convenient way to approach life. It allows you to do pretty much whatever you want without having to worry about violating pesky moral laws. But convenient as it may be, it's not grounded in reality.

Truth does exist. It's real, and it's eternal. It doesn't change from age to age, culture to culture, or person to person. It also isn't hard to know.

Of course, sin and all its effects can block our understanding of truth. It can also make us less willing to seek truth and order our lives around it. But if we seek it, we can find it. It's not hidden. God doesn't keep truth a secret from man. He wants us to know it, believe it, and live by it. Accordingly, He ensures that the truth about Himself, man, and the world is presented in Sacred Scripture and interpreted infallibly, without error, by the Catholic Church. That infallibility is guaranteed by the Holy Spirit, the Third Person of the Trinity.

There's not room in this book, let alone this chapter, to go into detail on all the truths of the Faith. But in general, the most fundamental truths are these:

First, God exists. He is a communion of three Persons, a family, sharing the same nature and giving themselves eternally to each other in love. He created the world, He loves the world, and He became man, dying on a cross and rising from the dead, so that man might spend eternity in heaven with Him. God cares. He's involved. He's generous. He's just. And He's merciful.

About man, about ourselves, we know this much. We are made in the image and likeness of God. We are both body and soul, and both have a great dignity. We have the capacity to love, to serve, and to choose good from evil. We have inherited a fallen human nature from the first man and first woman, and we bear in our souls the wounds of sin. But because of the cross, redemption is possible. Forgiveness is possible.

We also know both good and evil exist in this world. We know that virtue is beautiful and vice ugly. We know there is a moral law and a natural law. We know that what we do in this life matters: every action and every choice has a consequence. And we know there is purpose, there is a plan, there is love, and there is hope. In this life, there is always hope.

Those are the basic truths we need to bring to our analysis and use of the media.

FINER DISTINCTIONS
We also need to bring an understanding of the distinction between truth and accuracy, for they are not the same.

Sometimes truth and accuracy go together. If news reporting isn't accurate, it's not truthful. If our descriptions of our lives and ourselves on social networking sites or blogs contain inaccurate information, they are likewise not truthful. In these kinds of media, accuracy matters. The Church says as much in *Communio et Progressio*, writing:

> Modern man cannot do without information that is full, consistent, accurate and true. Without it, he cannot understand the perpetually changing world in which he lives nor be able to adapt himself to the real situation (CP 34).

But other forms of media don't have to be accurate to be truth-filled. In movies depicting historical events, the dialogue delivered by actors will likely be more passionate and articulate than the words that were spoken by the actual historical persons. Some events might be omitted or merged with other events, either to conform to the constraints of time or to enable more powerful storytelling. In dozens of ways, the media might not be strictly accurate, but it can still convey truth.[*]

---

[*] Further, Pope Paul VI emphasized the obligation of creative or imaginative media to be faithful

The same goes for the genres of science fiction or fantasy. Just because fairies and orcs and elves don't exist, doesn't mean movies about fairies and orcs and elves can't convey some deep truth about human existence. *Communio et Progressio* tells us:

> Even when the artist takes flight from the tangible and solid world and pursues his creative fantasies, he can give priceless insight into the human condition. Stories fashioned out of imagination in which the artist creates characters that live and evolve in a world of fiction, these too communicate their special truth. Even though they are not real, they are realistic; for they are made of the very stuff of human life. They even affect those deep causes that rouse men to blaze with life. For, in the light they throw on these causes, the sensitive man may know them for what they are. And with this knowledge he can begin to foresee the direction that humanity will take (CP 56).

The final thing we need to understand about the fourth media key is that not all truths media conveys must be pleasant. A news channel that only reported good news might be comforting to watch, but it wouldn't help us understand the world in which we live. Likewise, if movies and television shows only told nice stories about nice Christian people doing nice Christian things, their power to illuminate truth would be fairly limited. That's why the Church doesn't automatically frown upon media that depicts moral evil.

In *Inter Mirifica*, the Church explains that, "The chronicling, the description or the representation of moral evil can, with the help of the means of social communication and with suitable dramatization, lead to a deeper

---

to the truth: "To give graphic and dramatic expression to the finer things of life, to give 'life' to his creation, the artist is certainly entitled to draw on the resources of imagination. But fanciful creations, while not expected to portray concrete reality, must not, at the same time, deny this reality. Even they have an obligation of fidelity to the truth and to the values inseparable from it. True art, in fact, is one of the noblest human expressions of truth. Therefore, to give a real service to man and to be a true follower of the truth, the artist must help man in his search for truth and in his firm adhesion to it" (Message, Sixth Word Communications Day, April 21, 1972, no. 4).

knowledge and analysis of man and to a manifestation of the true and the good in all their splendor" (IM 7).

Communio et Progressio, quoting Pope Pius XII, gets even more specific:

> [H]uman life "certainly cannot be understood, at least when considering violent and serious conflicts, if one deliberately turns one's eyes from the crimes and evils from which they often have their origin. How then, can ideal films take this as their subject?...When the conflict with evil, not excluding cases when evil prevails for a while, is treated within the context of a work as a whole, in an effort to understand life better, to see how it should be ordered, or to show how man should conduct himself, how he should think and act with more consistency, then, in such cases, such matter can be chosen as an integral part of the development of the whole film." Such a work would contribute to moral progress (CP 57).[33]

But what does that kind of work look like in practice?

Proclaiming Truth: Illustrating the Fourth Media Key

SEEING TRUTH

On film it looks a lot like Steven Spielberg's *Schindler's List*. The 1993 film seeks to present the truth about the Holocaust and one man's fight to save Jewish lives. And the story it tells is indeed filled with truth. Not only does it tell the true story of what Oskar Schindler—a German factory owner during the Second World War—did to save the lives of his Jewish employees, but it also reveals the truth about how deeply original sin has wounded man. It shows the atrocities that we are capable of committing in our fallen condition. Yet, it also shows that redemption is possible, that men can do good in the face of evil, and that God has not abandoned us. The movie is filled with fundamental truths about God, man, and the world. It reveals truth.

But strictly speaking, the movie is not accurate.

When Schindler watched the slaughter in the Krakow Ghetto, there was no dramatic soundtrack playing in the background. When he first moved to Poland, he didn't charm all the German high officials in one night. His real conversations with Amon Goeth, Itzac Stern, and the Jews who worked for him sounded little like the dialogue from the screenplay. Some facts about his efforts were left out, and the details of others changed. And yet even the inaccurate elements of the film convey truth. They reveal, in the heightened manner appropriate to the cinematic arts the drama, the danger and the glory of Schindler's secret crusade to save Jewish lives.

Schindler's List isn't a nice film. It's not pleasant to watch. It's utterly brutal in its depiction of what the Jews suffered. The ashes of burned human bodies fall from the sky. Soldiers randomly shoot children. And men and women's bodies are photographed like the pieces of meat Nazis believed them to be. The film is dark, even savage at times. But because of that savagery, we're able to more fully grasp the horror of what man did.

Schindler's List isn't a movie for children. It's also not a perfect movie. While some of the nudity in the movie is integral to the story being told—such as Nazis stripping Jewish women before sending them into the showers at Auschwitz—the story could perhaps have been told just as powerfully without a rather graphic sex scene and a few other gratuitous shots of women's bodies. Scenes such as those can harm the viewers, as well as those involved in the actual production. Nonetheless, *Schindler's List* still made it on to the Vatican's 1995 list of 45 "important films"—films that in someway exemplify what media, what moviemaking, is supposed to be about. *Schindler's List* is there because it illuminates truth through the story it tells.

Other films, however, have done just the opposite. They base themselves on a lie, and use the dramatic arts to make that lie more convincing.

Schindler's List's polar opposite, the award-winning *Atonement*, was released in 2008. Although the movie was based on a fictional book, it was set in the context of real events—World War II and the plight of wartime London. There was truth in the film—true battles, true suffering, true tragedy. But the heart of the film was a lie. While *Schindler's List* illuminated the possibility of redemption, *Atonement* denied that possibility. It denied mercy, forgiveness, and salvation.

The movie itself tells the tale of Briony Tallis, a wealthy young English girl who, as a child, mistakenly accuses her sister Cecilia's lover, Robbie, of a terrible crime. The lovers are separated, first when Robbie is thrown into prison, and later when he goes to fight in France. Despite the horrors of war, the two lovers are reunited, with one of the final scenes of the movie showing the two back together, happy, in love, and confident that Robbie will be vindicated. They believe that because, in the intervening years, Briony both concluded she was wrong to accuse Robbie and discovered the identity of the real criminal. They ask her to go to her parents and the authorities and tell them the truth, and she agrees. Briony's opportunity to atone for her mistake and put things right has finally come.

But that opportunity is a fiction. The movie ends with a much older Briony, now a famous author, giving a televised interview about her latest book, the book that tells the story of her childhood tragedy. Cecilia and Robbie's reunion, she confesses, never happened. In reality, Robbie died in Dunkirk, and her sister during the Blitz. The two were never reunited. It was a fiction she invented so that the book might have a "happy ending." In reality, her wrong was never atoned for. It never could be atoned for. For her there could never be forgiveness or redemption. The movie asserts that atonement, grace, and hope are just illusions we cling to in order to avoid seeing the sorry state of our lives.

The movie is well-acted, the scenery and costume designs lush, the cinematography first-rate. It's a well-made and visually beautiful film. But that can't compensate for the ugliness of the lie it tells. *Atonement* doesn't illuminate the human condition. It doesn't reveal truth about God, man, and the world. It obscures truth. And because of that, it fails as media.

SPEAKING TRUTH

As with the other media keys, the fourth media key isn't just about the films and television shows we watch. It's also about keeping truth at the heart of the media we make and use. In the world of blogs, podcasts, social networking sites, and online forums, we all, at least potentially, are media-makers. We can all "make" media that leads people to the truth, and we can all use media in a way that obscures truth.

We "make" media that leads people to the truth when we use our blogs or Facebook pages not just to gossip or report on the more mundane aspects of our life, but to talk about what really matters to us and why. Our blog can be a vehicle for articulating our struggles with the culture, our questions about the Faith, or our journey to God. In online forums we can evangelize, and on social networking sites we can post interesting articles about faith or culture that can spark discussions among friends from various viewpoints. Even posting pictures of our children on a social networking site can communicate some of the truth about Catholic family life. In all those ways, our use of the social media reflects and promotes an understanding of truth.

But those forms of media also make it particularly easy to let lies, both big and small, worm their way into our use. There are the obvious lies, the lies that began this chapter, designing avatars or online personas that have no grounding in who we really are. But there are plenty of lesser lies we can tell without pretending to be of a different, sex, race, or species.

For example, it's for good reason that Facebook has earned the nickname "Fakebook." All too often the profiles we devise for ourselves don't represent who we are, but who we want people to think we are. We can leave out the details we don't like, overemphasize the ones we do, and present to the world an idealized and ultimately false picture of our life. [34]

In online forums and chat rooms, it's equally possible to mask our identities, as well as to do or say things we would never do in real life (like hurl insults at a perfect stranger). The Internet affords an anonymity that can embolden us to violate charity. It's easy to throw out insults or spread malicious gossip when we can't see the pain our words inflict.

It's also easy to cheat. Several years ago, one British professor characterized higher education in the UK as a "cut and paste culture." Those same words can just as easily be applied to the U.S. Thanks to the vast amount of content easily searchable online, not only can students copy and paste passages from articles they read into their own Word documents, but they also can purchase ready-made research papers from websites like essayprofessors.com. According to a 2005 Duke University study, at least 40 percent of America's college students admit to passing off material they found online as their own. And by now, that number is likely much higher.[35]

Whether we're creating a misleading picture of our life on Facebook, cultivating an online persona who does what we would never do offline, or simply failing to give credit where credit is due, we're not using the media in a way that reflects or upholds truth. We're not using media as we're supposed to use it. We're not being true to our call as Christians. And that's a problem.

Truth through Beauty: Why Truth-Filled Media Matters

As we've talked about in previous chapters, the media, with all its images, sounds, and cinematic nuance, can reach our hearts and minds in a uniquely powerful way. Because of that power, it's important that the messages being communicated are truthful.

The media, the Church tells us, can make truth more compelling: "The communication of truth can have a redemptive power," says *Aetatis*

Novae, the pastoral instruction released to commemorate the twentieth anniversary of *Communio et Progressio*.[†]

But the media can also make lies more believable.

As my colleague and friend, Franciscan University theatre professor Shawn Dougherty, said in a 2009 interview, "Jesus used the parables to teach people because story is an incredibly powerful tool. If I can make you sympathize with a character in a movie or a play, and later you discover that character is homosexual, you're forced to rethink your ideas about homosexuals."[36]

The nature of our culture makes the power of storytelling through media all the greater. But what can work against us can also work for us. We live in an age where absolutes are frowned upon. Moralists are frowned upon as well. People don't want to be preached at. And when they hear moralists preaching, hearts and minds quickly close. They don't want to be told about Truth—the kind with a capital T. Media, however, offers us a way around that problem.

Through media, truth can be woven into a movie, a song, a video game, even a Facebook page. It can be made part of a story. And the story can do what we can't. It can connect with people on the level of emotion. It can attract them to beauty, to goodness, to truth by engaging them in the story. In a far less didactic way, media can lead people to the ends our preaching can't. It catches people off their guard, shining a light on truths they didn't know existed and in times and places where they weren't expecting to find them. And for that, it's all the more effective.

Truth in our own use of media matters, at least on some level, in a similar manner. Pope Paul VI once said that the best teachers of the Faith are the best witnesses to the Faith.[‡] And we can't be good witnesses to

---

[†] Pontifical Council on Social Communications, Pastoral Instruction on Social Communications on the Twentieth Anniversary of *Communio et Progressio, Aetatis Novae* (February 22, 1992), 6. Available at www.vatican.va/roman_curia/pontifical_councils/pccs (hereafter cited in text as AN).

[‡] "Modern man listens more willingly to witnesses than to teachers, and if he does listen to teachers, it is because they are witnesses." Paul VI, Apostolic Exhortation *Evangelii Nuntiandi* (December 8,

Christ if we're lying about our lives on Facebook or copying papers off the Internet. We can't illuminate truth for others if we can't live truth in our own lives. We also can't know ourselves or give of ourselves if we're not being ourselves.

Some authors have argued that creating multiple identities for oneself on the Internet is actually a good thing. In the book *Cyber Rules: What You Really Need to Know About the Internet*, the editors argue that men pretending to be women or women pretending to be cats can help us get to know ourselves better. The Internet, they contend, allows us to try out alternate behaviors or personas in a "risk free" environment. The teenagers who do this, they write, "gain insight and appreciation for their identities. Maybe we can learn something from them."

However, they also note that, "With children and teenagers who experiment with new and different identities online, the offline effects may be more intense because they are at a very critical stage of development. If, as the research suggests, over half of teenagers regularly lie about themselves online, this propensity may begin to show up offline."[37]

That latter statement seems a bit closer to the mark, especially because there is no such thing as a "risk free" environment—at least, not in the way proponents of such behavior claim there is. Those arguments are based on the idea that the choices we make in the virtual world have no affect on who we are in the real world. They presume a division of body and soul that just doesn't exist. In truth, the choices we make are the choices we make, regardless of whether we make them online through an avatar or in the real world through our bodies.

Virtual worlds and social media may allow us to experiment with identities and fine-tune how we represent ourselves to others. But compared to the more old-fashioned methods of self-discovery—contemplation, reflection, and dialog with a trusted individual—they don't really help us to know ourselves any better. It's a safe bet that your average six-year-old

---

1975), 41. Available at www.vatican.va/holy_father/paul_vi (hereafter cited in text as EN).

learns more about himself (and the repercussions for his behavior) sitting in the corner, than he could designing the virtual character of his dreams when playing *Buzz Lightyear: Operation Alien Rescue.* And the same truth applies to adults. We come to know ourselves by finding ourselves in Christ, not by pretending to be a club-going Goth in Second Life.

Applying the Fourth Media Key

STEP 1: PRAY
Pray for the cardinal virtue of fortitude.

Fortitude, the *Catechism* says, "is the moral virtue that ensures firmness in difficulties and constancy in the pursuit of the good. It strengthens the resolve to resist temptations and to overcome obstacles in the moral life. The virtue of fortitude enables one to conquer fear, even fear of death, and to face trials and persecutions. It disposes one even to renounce and sacrifice his life in defense of a just cause" (CCC 1808).

STEP 2: RESEARCH
You know the drill. Google it. Read about it. Ask about it. Talk about it. As often as possible, know what you're getting yourself into before you watch, use, or play any new media. Be aware of what truths or lies the media proclaims from the outset, and reflect on the distinction between accuracy and truth before you enter into conversations with others about media.

STEP 3: ASK QUESTIONS
1. What philosophies or ideologies does this media focus on? Are those philosophies proposed positively, negatively, or ambivalently?

2. What is the underlying message of this media? Does it conform to a Catholic understanding of reality?

3. Do the characters' actions conform to or reject truth? What consequences are attached to their following or rejecting truth?

4. Does accuracy matter to this particular form of media? If so, is the media accurate? If not, do the inaccuracies enhance or compromise the truth?

5. Does the media depict moral evil? If so, how is it depicted? What is the purpose of its depiction? Does it glamorize evil or does it help illuminate the tragedy of the fallen human condition?

6. Do I ever do or say anything through media that I would not do or say in person? If so, should I be doing it or saying it?

7. Am I honest in my portrayal of myself online? If not, why am I less than honest?

8. Do I use avatars or play games where I can develop characters very different from myself? Why do I do this? What do I think I gain from this?

9. Do I create media or use media in such a way that it helps people understand the truth about Christ?

10. How does my behavior online affect the way I think and act when I am not online?

STEP 4: INTEGRATION

☛ Use your blog or Facebook page to post links to interesting articles about the Faith and culture and to challenge prevailing cultural norms that deviate from the Truth.

☛ Don't shy away from difficult discussions about God or morality in online forums.

☛ Never misrepresent yourself on social networking sites, in Internet chat rooms, or other online media. This doesn't mean you shouldn't be discerning and prudent about the personal information you share online. You should. But there is a difference between keeping parts of your life private and misleading people about who you really are.

- Never use the Internet to pass off another's work as your own.
- Exercise the same charity towards others online that you would in person.
- Practice what Pope John Paul II urged all of us to do with media—movies, television shows, online clips, video games— that obfuscates truth: make your voice heard that you disapprove of and do not intend to support such media. Speak out about it to friends, writers, and even the media-makers and distributors themselves.

STEP 5: PASSING IT ON

- After watching a movie or a show with your children or students, ask them to identify the truths and/or lies promoted by the film. Point out to them those they can't see, and talk about why certain messages are true and others false.
- Ask them the same questions about media you ask yourself.
- Discourage participation in online communities that encourage users to have false identities.
- Encourage them to spend quiet time alone with God, including in Eucharistic adoration.
- Help them find sites created for their demographic about the Catholic faith.
- Lovingly monitor their Facebook page or blog and question them if something seems less than true.

The fourth media key reminds us that there is no real or lasting happiness in lies. There is no freedom in lies. There is no life in lies. All those things can only be found in Christ, who is "the way, and *the truth*, and *the life*"

(Jn. 14:6). The fourth media key also calls us to be aware of the truth and the lies in the media we watch, and to model and live the truth in all the different ways we use the media. When we do that, we're taking an important step towards wielding the fifth media key. We inspire.

Chapter Six

O━┓

Inspiring
The Fifth Media Key

As anyone who has ever driven through Pittsburgh, Pennsylvania can attest, making your way from one point in the city to another can be something of a challenge.

Built along three rivers and situated in the midst of massive hills, the city is chock full of bridges, overpasses, and interchanges, not to mention one-way streets that form triangular, not rectangular, blocks. Distinguishing one bridge from the next, let alone knowing which connector road to take, can be daunting even for life-long residents of the city.

Fortunately, in recent years, Pittsburgh has taken pity on the poor drivers attempting to efficiently navigate their way through the city and posted better road signs throughout. As long as you keep your eyes peeled for signs to Oakland, the South Side, and the North Shore, you can reach your destination without nearly so many "detours" as used to be the norm. The signs point the way.

In some ways, getting to heaven is a lot like getting around Pittsburgh. We're often not sure of the road we need to take. Obstacles even more daunting than rivers and mountains stand in our way. And it is so very easy to take the wrong exit and suddenly find ourselves miles away from where we need to be.

This is why God, like Pittsburgh's city government, has also given us signs: signs that point the way to heaven, signs that point the way to Him. And media is one of those signs.

In the Pontifical Council for Social Communication's document "Ethics in Internet," the Church writes:

> Today it takes no great stretch of the imagination to envisage the earth as an interconnected globe humming with electronic transmissions—a chattering planet nestled in the provident silence of space. The ethical question is whether this is contributing to authentic human development and helping individuals and peoples to be true to their transcendent destiny (EI 1).

That last sentence is key. There, the Church tells us that the value of the media revolution hinges on the answer to one question: Is it helping us to be true to our "transcendent destiny"? In other words, is it helping us get to heaven? Is it a sign, pointing the way to God? If the answer is yes, then the media fulfills the fifth media key: it inspires us to the good.

"God Breathed" Media: Understanding the Fifth Media Key

The world we live in is full of signs pointing the way to God. Some of those signs—like the order and beauty of nature—are built into creation. Other signs—such as music, art, and architecture—are made by us, with God's help. We create those signs, and through them, people find their way. Media belongs to that class of signs. By God's grace, we make media that inspires people towards their transcendent destiny.

The Congregation for Catholic Education describes the help God has given us, writing:

God, the Supreme Good, incessantly communicates his gifts to men and women, the objects of his particular solicitude and love, in anticipation of the time when he will communicate himself more fully to them in the beatific vision. More than that: in order that his image in his human creatures might increasingly reflect the divine perfection (cf. Mt. 5, 48), he has willed to associate them in his own work, making them, in their turn, messengers and dispensers of the same gifts to their brothers and sisters and to all humanity (TFP 1).

That passage tells us that through the media, we share in God's work of communicating love to others. It also tells us that God helped man to develop media so that we could use it to inspire people to pursue virtue and a relationship with Him. Simply put, it tells us media exists to be a sign pointing the way to holiness.

While the word "inspiring" can conjure up images of Hallmark cards, Lifetime movies, and overly sentimental Christian fiction, the fifth media key does not mean media needs to be cheesy or hokey. There's nothing wishy-washy about true inspiration. And that's because there's nothing wishy-washy about the Holy Spirit.

The root of "inspires" is the Latin *inspirare*, which literally means "to breath into." Breath is the literal meaning of the Greek *pneuma,* which also translates as "spirit." Accordingly, in both Greek and Latin translations of Sacred Scripture, the Holy Spirit is literally called the "breath of God." It is the Holy Spirit who inspired the Biblical authors to write what they wrote (2 Tim. 3:16). It is the Holy Spirit who teaches us all things (Jn. 14:26). And it is the Holy Spirit who gives us the power to witness, communicate, comfort, and heal (Acts 1:8, 2:4, 9:31, 10:38).

What the Holy Spirit does in us, is, to a certain extent, what media should do in all those it touches. It should breathe into people a desire for understanding, wisdom, and virtue. It should enlighten and raise questions. It should point beyond itself to something greater, something bigger.

Good media, like good road signs, assumes we are on a journey. It assumes that we don't want to stay where we are or end up in the wrong place. It also knows that its job is to help us get where we need to go, to help us move forward.

Sometimes media does that by holding up a mirror to the culture and the human condition. It shows us where we are in order to inspire us to question our current state or aim for a better destination. At other times, it shows us where we want to go. It inspires us to action by revealing how great things are a little further along on the journey. Media can also directly or indirectly give us instructions for the journey, showing or telling us the steps we need to take to move forward. That's media at is best.

And media at its worst?

Like an arrow pointing traffic in the wrong direction, media at its worst points us in the wrong direction. It misleads us, confuses us, and tells us to take a route that's not only wrong but perilous. It "inspires," but not in the "God-breathed" kind of way, taking us off the road to sanctity and putting us on the road to perdition.

That kind of media, Pope John Paul II wrote, has "the capacity to do grave harm...by presenting an inadequate or even deformed outlook on life, on the family, on religion and on morality." *

As Christians seeking holiness, we need to rely on the fifth media key to direct us towards media and uses of media that inspire us towards the true, the good, and the beautiful. We also need to rely on it to direct us away from media that inspires us towards the false, the evil, and the ugly. The Church tells us as much in *Inter Mirifica*, writing:

All who, of their own free choice, make use of these media of communications as readers, viewers or listeners have special obligations. For a proper

---

* John Paul II, 38th World Communications Day Message *The Media and the Family: A Risk and a Richness* (January 24, 2004), 2. Available at www.vatican.va/holy_father/john_paul_ii (hereafter cited in text as MF).

choice demands that they fully favor those presentations that are out-standing for their moral goodness, their knowledge and their artistic or technical merit. They ought, however, to avoid those that may be a cause or occasion of spiritual harm to themselves, or that can lead others into danger through base example, or that hinder desirable presentations and promote those that are evil (IM 9).

Pointing the Way: Illustrating the Fifth Media Key

GOOD DIRECTIONS

Topping the list of the all time greatest inspirational movies may be the Frank Capra classic, *It's a Wonderful Life*. Filmed in 1946, just one year after the end of World War II, the movie follows the life of George Bailey, a young man from a small town who sacrifices his own dreams to help those he loves. When tragedy strikes, Bailey questions the worth of those sacrifices and his life in general. That questioning leads to despair and near suicide. Then an angel intervenes.

That angel, Clarence, gives George a glimpse of what the world would have been like without him. He shows George how all the small acts of good he did—pulling his brother out of an icy pond as a child, preventing a grief-stricken pharmacist from giving out the wrong prescription, using his own money to bolster up his father's failing business—bore fruit not just in a few lives, but in hundreds. That glimpse restores George's faith and trust in God's plan. It puts him back on the road to heaven.

The movie does the same for its viewers. At the time *It's a Wonderful Life* was made, there were a lot of George Bailey's in America and around the world. Men, women, and children across the globe were reeling from the devastation of the Second World War, the loss of tens of millions of lives, and the murder of more than six million Jews. The world seemed a cruel, crazy, and chaotic place, and the question of what all the dying had been for wasn't far from anyone's mind.

Accordingly, when the script for *It's a Wonderful Life* came across Capra's desk, he jumped at the chance to make the movie. A devout Catholic, Capra later told one interviewer that he "made it to combat the modern trend towards atheism." He wanted to remind people that there was a purpose and a plan, that their sacrifices had mattered, and that one person can make a difference. He wanted the film to inspire people to believe again.[38]

If the number of times a movie is shown on Christmas Eve is any indicator, Capra's film does just that. Every Christmas, millions of people around the globe wrap up their Christmas Eve watching *It's a Wonderful Life*, which has blanketed the Christmas airwaves for more than 40 years. They watch it for the fifth, tenth, or twentieth time because the reminder the angel gives George—a reminder to trust, love, and believe—is a reminder they need as well. They watch it knowing they'll walk away inspired, their desire to pursue the right path strengthened and renewed.

Not all inspirational movies, however, are Christmas Eve fare. Inspirational movies can also be complex, even dark. Nor do they need to deliver pat answers to the questions they raise. They can inspire us simply by getting us to ask the questions. Christopher Nolan's two Batman flicks, *Batman Begins* and *The Dark Night*, have not an angel in sight, yet both have within them the ability to truly inspire people to the good thanks to the tough questions they raise about the struggle between good and evil.

In one particularly powerful scene from the second film, Batman's nemesis, the Joker, sets out to prove that people are inherently evil and that chaos is the organizing theme of the universe. He does this by taking two commuter ferries hostage. The Joker promises the passengers on each ferry that they can save themselves by simply pushing a button that will detonate the explosives on the other ferry. As the passengers debate what they will do, the movie indirectly asks its audience to take a side. What will the passengers choose? Who is right? The Joker? Or Batman, who believes in order and goodness? The more perceptive viewers might also find themselves asking, "What would I do? Would I sacrifice the lives of others so that I might live? Or would I rather die than harm another?"

Both *Batman* movies end on a note of hope. Evil is still evil—dark, present, and unrelenting—but good triumphs. In those movies it's possible for people to overcome their fallen human nature and embrace righteousness. They inspire us not only to question, but to believe that hope still exists for this fallen world.

BAD DIRECTIONS
But that note of hope is absent from much of what passes for Hollywood's "best." In tinsel town, it often seems as if the most surefire way to win an Academy Award is to make a film devoid of hope, devoid of light. That's nihilism, one of the most common philosophies employed in film to point people in the wrong direction.

In 1992, Clint Eastwood's *Unforgiven* swept the Oscars, picking up statues for Best Supporting Actor, Best Editing, Best Director, and Best Picture. The movie told the tale of retired gunslinger William Munney, who thought he had found redemption from his murderous past in the love of his wife and a quiet farming life. He thought he had become a different man. But when put to the test, the film tells us that Munney thought wrong. He not only kills a young man for money, but he also quickly and coolly dispenses of an entire saloon full of cowboys and deputies when the need to take revenge strikes. His redemption, the film tells us, was just an illusion. He remains unredeemed, unforgiven, because nothing else is truly possible.

The last scene of *Unforgiven* features Munney standing at his wife's grave, the brown and empty plains of Kansas stretching out all around him, devoid of life, devoid of hope. In that moment, there are no questions for the viewer to ask, no good for which to strive. There is only despair.

Unforgiven, for all its technical merit, fails because it fails to inspire to the good. It kills hope, rather than gives hope. Other movies have failed to inspire in equally dangerous ways.

For example, in 1997, a fourteen-year-old boy in Kentucky, charged with killing three of his classmates, told police he got the idea from the film *The Basketball Diaries*, which featured a dream sequence in which a student guns down five classmates and his teacher. Did the movie make the boy shoot his classmates? No, not at all. But it did point an already misguided soul further along the wrong path. With its stylized images of violence, it held up a false picture of reality, a reality where taking life is "cool" and revenge just. It did not give viewers true and right directions.[39]

That failing also holds true for just about any modern "coming of age" sexual comedy. By depicting teens' sexual antics as hip and by making illicit relations the focal point of the action, movies such as *Bart Got a Room* and *American Pie* can confuse teenagers about what relationships are supposed to look like, why chastity matters, and what is and is not cool to do. They can inspire them to misuse their bodies and the bodies of others.

Essentially, how inspiring a film is comes down to whether or not it itself is inspired by the third and fourth media keys. John Paul II explains, "Communication in any form must always be inspired by the ethical criterion of respect for the truth and for the dignity of the human person" (MF 2). *It's a Wonderful Life* and *Batman* were so inspired. *Unforgiven* and countless other movies were not.

VIRTUAL DIRECTIONS

That same criteria determines how inspiring other forms of media are: Do they respect the human person and do they respect the truth?[†]

---

† "The modern media are addressed not only to society in general, but most of all to families, to young people and also to very young children. What "way" do the media point out? What 'truth' do they propose? What 'life' do they offer? This is of concern not only to Christians, but to all people of good will" (John Paul II, Message, 31st World Communications Day, 1997, no. 7).

For the Catholic teen and young adult website, PhatMass.com, the answer is a definitive "yes."

Launched in 2000, PhatMass employs just about every type of Web-based technology around—from forums and YouTube videos to blog sites and Facebook—to connect with its target audience. The overarching theme of all posts, links, and videos is definitely "all things Catholic," but without any saccharine or overly pious talk. Both faithful and focused on plugging young Catholics into a community of likeminded peers, the website gives young people information about the Church and culture, links them together in a virtual world, and ultimately inspires them to live more faithful lives. Its whole purpose is, in fact, inspiration. The website's mission is to be a sign pointing the way to heaven.

Then, there's FreethinkingTeens.com.

Like PhatMass, FreeThinkingTeens employs all the latest and greatest Web technology. There are podcasts, forums, blogs, and more on the site. It is designed to engage, and it does. But like that road sign with the arrow pointing in the wrong direction, FreeThinkingTeen aims to lead young people away from God. Its mission is to promote atheism. From posting powerful diatribes against God to sponsoring a Blaspheme the Holy Spirit Competition, the website's creators do everything they can to get teens off the road to heaven and on to a very different path. They work hard to inspire teens...just in the wrong direction.

Social networking sites such as Facebook have the same potential to point people in the right direction or the wrong one. Over the years, I've witnessed students use their Facebook pages to post links to stories about the Faith, engage their non-believing high school friends in debate, and display videos they've made about prayer, the saints, and missions work. Others use Facebook to spread the word about good charitable organizations, raise money for cancer research, or spark discussions about controversial issues like abortion. For them, social networking sites aren't primarily about spying on classmates or accumulating as many "friends" as possible. They're not a forum for self-display or a place to garner attention. They're tools to inspire people to a fuller, richer way of life. And when their activity on those sites is inspired by a respect for truth and the dignity of the human person, they do just that. When that respect is missing, so is the inspiration.

GAMING DIRECTIONS

And what about video games? Can they employ the "inspiring" key, or do all games fall short in this regard? The answer is, "Yes, video games can be inspiring," but with some qualifications, given the crop of video games produced to date.

There's no getting around the body of evidence that suggests a correlation between violent video games and real life violence. Studies continue to demonstrate that violent video games can contribute to pro-violent attitudes and hostile personalities, as well as less forgiving and aggressive behavior.[40]

Those tendencies seem to be particularly acute when the video game has a narrative or story component to it. A researcher explained:

> When story was present, game players felt greater identification, sense of presence, and physiological arousal...Addition of a narrative function to provide justification, increase arousal, and therefore increase learning. It provides frequent exposure to violent behavior committed under the direction of the game player by a character with whom the player closely identifies, which is likely to increase facilitation and this inhibition. It increases the experience of positive emotion, which may further desensitize the viewer to violent behavior.[41]

That's not to say that all video games containing some element of violence are inherently bad. God calls all men and women to defend the good against evil, and just as films (e.g. the *Lord of the Rings* movies) can reinforce the importance of this call, so can some video games. They can do that when the "character" clearly fights evil and progresses in the game due to his display of virtue.

Two examples that come close to this are *Freedom Force* and its sequel, *Freedom Force vs. The 3rd Reich*, where players guide a team of superheroes as they defend Patriot City against "the planet's worst miscreants"—a horde of crooks, super-powered gangsters, aliens, robots, and Nazi villains. The lines between good and evil are clearly delineated, and the player is encouraged to protect innocent civilians, rescue captured heroes and citizens, free hostages, and stop the misanthropic felons from damaging the city. Flight simulators, which allow players to take on the role of Royal Air Force Pilots in the Battle of Britain, can also do this.

Unfortunately, games like these are few and far between. "Unfortunately," not only because most games inspire more to vice than virtue, but because of the very research cited above. If an immersion in the story of a video game can "increase learning" and change behavior accordingly, then video games should be able to influence behavior positively as well as negatively. One could argue that the problem with video games is not so much that too many videos games fail to inspire toward the good, but rather that we've not come close to exploring the possibilities and potential of this medium. More conscious and concerted efforts need to be directed towards creating video games that engage, entertain, and inspire virtuous moral choices.[42] Like other forms of media, video games should be able to inspire men and women, boys and girls to the good. If they are truth-filled and affirm human dignity, games should be able to inspire virtue, not vice. But for now, that remains a mostly unrealized potential. And again, that is unfortunate, because that's what media, all media, is supposed to do.

Reaching Our Destination:
Why the Fifth Media Key Matters

Media, of course, doesn't *have* to be inspiring. It doesn't have to point the way to God or anything else for that matter. It can be as uninspired as a game of online solitaire. Uninspiring media is still media. It's just not good media. It's like a tool left out in the yard to rust and rot. It's not serving its true purpose. It's not pointing people anywhere.

Media should inspire because that's what media is intended to do. It's media's reason for existence. It's its ontological purpose. The Church considers media a "gift from God" because of what media can help people accomplish. It calls it a "marvelous thing" because it can "provide inspiration, encouragement...attract people to a fuller experience of the life of faith, and enrich the religious lives of users."[43]

The fifth media key encourages us to expect the best from media. It draws a clear line in the sand between media being used for its true purpose—to direct us to all that's good, true, and beautiful—and media that either misdirects us or wastes its potential by directing us nowhere. It also gives us a guidepost for our own use of the media. It reminds us that there is more to media than simply being entertained or killing time. It challenges us to use media to inspire and be inspired, to draw closer to God and draw others closer to Him as well.

Life is short. God gives us only so much time to learn and to love. And one day, we'll have to answer for what we did with that time. We'll have to answer for the media we've invested hours of our life watching, playing, using, and making.

That doesn't mean we need to devote every single second of the time we spend using media time to doing apostolate work. Remember what the Church tells us in *Communio et Progressio*: "A proper balance must be kept, not only between hard news, educational material, and entertainment, but also between the light and more serious forms of entertainment" (CP 16).

God wants us to enjoy life, to laugh, experience joy, and play, and media can be a part of that. Nevertheless, that enjoyment, that play, should still in some way lead us closer to Him. It should help us understand God or ourselves a little better. It should help us think a little more deeply or clearly, and move a bit closer to our transcendent destiny.

A good comedy can do that. A video game can do that. Participating in an online forum can do that. Growing in holiness doesn't have to be boring work. In many ways, nobody has more fun than the saints. Sin breeds sadness, eternal sadness. Conversely, the further you get from sin, the happier you are. That's why ultimately, the only real fun is that which doesn't get in the way of our journey to heaven. The rest is just an illusion.

Applying the Fifth Media Key

STEP 1: PRAY

Pray for the theological virtue of hope to be integrated into all media, including your own use of the media.

> "Hope is the theological virtue by which we desire the kingdom of heaven and eternal life as our happiness, placing our trust in Christ's promises and relying not on our own strength, but on the help of the grace of the Holy Spirit. 'Let us hold fast the confession of our hope without wavering, for he who promised is faithful.' 'The Holy Spirit...he poured out upon us richly through Jesus Christ our Savior, so that we might be justified by his grace and become heirs in hope of eternal life'"(CCC 1817).

STEP 2: RESEARCH

The goal: find out what the aim—the mission, the vision, the purpose—of a particular piece of media is. Try to understand where the media is trying to lead people. The means, the same as always: Google. Read. Talk.

STEP 3: ASK QUESTIONS

1. Does this media inspire me to reflect upon and seek greater understanding of God, the world, or my own life?

2. Does it inspire me to ask questions about things that matter?

3. Does it inspire me to talk with others about the questions or issues it raises and share what I've experienced?

4. Does it inspire me to action? If so, what kind of action?

5. Does it inspire understanding for the experiences of others?

6. Does this media inspire me to hope or to despair?

7. How much time do I spend viewing or using media that doesn't inspire me to good ends? How does that affect me?

8. How much time do I spend viewing or using media that serves no end at all? How does that affect me?

9. How has media directed me to good ends in the past? How has it misdirected me?

10. Am I using social media to inspire others? If so, how? If not, why not?

STEP 4: INTEGRATION

- Avoid media that aims to misdirect you.

- Initiate conversations with friends about the video games you play or the movies and television shows you watch, then share with your friends how that media affected you.

- Talk with friends about films, shows, and games you've watched or played together. Ask each other questions that you think the media raises, and talk about how you can embrace or reject the directions it gives.

- Feature a running list on your blog, Facebook page, or webpage of what's inspiring you to live a holier and happier life. That list could include films, music, television, shows, books, video games, or even a beautiful piece of art.

- Post or email links to articles or songs that you think will inspire others to reflection or conversation. When you email or post that link, ask people what they think about it.

- Avoid using media just to "kill time."

STEP 5: PASSING IT ON

- Watch or use media with your children, and talk to them about how it inspires you.

- Ask your children the same questions you ask yourself when you watch and use media.

- Share with your children age-appropriate favorite films or music that has inspired you. Tell them about the first time you encountered that media and why it means so much to you.

- Ask your children what's inspiring them. Watch it, listen to it, or use it, then talk with them about how the media affected you.

- Send your teen a weekly text-message or email with a powerful quote from a saint, a pope, or a favorite writer. Then read about that saint or writer together.

Our job in life is to get ourselves (and our spouse and children if we have them) to heaven. God does most of the work for us, but we still have our part to play. Playing that part involves following the right directions and following them well. The fifth media key helps us to use media to do that. It helps us both distinguish good directions from bad in the media we encounter, and give others good directions that they can safely follow.

It keeps us on track, so that our journey to God doesn't veer off course, down the wide road and away from the narrow road (Mt. 7:14).

Even the most accurate directions, however, are only as good as the format in which they're delivered. Illegible directions or signs that don't capture our attention are of limited value. Hence the sixth media key: skillfully developed.

Chapter Seven

Skillfully Developed
The Sixth Media Key

It's what matters most to Hollywood. Every year at the granddaddy of all movie awards shows, the Academy Awards, Hollywood's elite turn out to honor the "best" in film. And by "best" they mean the most skillfully developed—the films with the most professional editing, convincing acting, thoughtful directing, and engaging writing. Lighting, costume design, makeup, camera work, and special effects: those are the measures of merit for film industry executives and power players.

Those are also the measures of merit for most movie critics and reviewers. A film earns one, two, three, or four stars based not on how true it is or how inspiring it is, but rather on how well-made it is. When Roger Ebert sits down to review a film, he's not looking at whether the producers upheld human dignity; he's looking for sensitive, intelligent, compelling, and artistic storytelling.

What matters to Hollywood likewise matters to Web designers, software engineers, video game developers, and virtually everyone else who earns their living by way of the secular media. If they want to attract users, sell games, and basically keep their jobs, the media they create and market must be skillfully developed. It must conform to industry standards for what does and does not constitute well-made media.

Those standards, believe it or not, also matter to the Church. The Church, like Hollywood, believes media should be skillfully developed.

In *Communio et Progressio*, the Catholic Church makes it clear that the spirit behind the media is important:

> Whoever wants to see the media take their allotted place in the history of Creation, in the Incarnation and Redemption, and to consider the morality that governs their use, must have a full and proper understanding of man (CP 15).

But the Church also makes it clear that something else is needed. Simply making media that's grounded in a true understanding of man and the world isn't enough. *Communio et Progressio* continues:

> He must also have a sound knowledge both of the true nature of social communication and of the tools at its service. 'Communicators' are all those who actively employ the media. These have a duty in conscience to make themselves competent in the art of social communication in order to be effective in their work. And as a man's influence on the process of communication grows, so does this duty (CP 15).

The Church's priorities and the media industry's priorities are not the same. Skillfully developed isn't the first media key for the Church; it's the sixth. It's not the foundation upon which everything else rests, as it is for Hollywood. But it's still a necessary ingredient for good media. And we need to remember this as we evaluate media, recommend media, and make media.

Careful Craftsmanship: Understanding the Sixth Media Key

Because skillfully developed media is what matters most to the media industry, this key is, in some ways, the easiest for us to understand. Our media-saturated environment has made most of us critics already, telling us what makes for well-made, well-designed media and bringing us into an encounter with examples of skillfully developed media virtually every day. By now, most of us are used to saying, 'The acting was terrible," "Those special effects were amazing," or "That website was not user friendly."

The knowledge we've acquired, the ability to form judgments about whether or not media is well-made, still serves us when we evaluate media from a Catholic standpoint. That's because when it comes to what constitutes skillfully developed media, the culture, not the Magisterium, is the ultimate judge. The Church's expertise is truth, not camera angles, and the Church knows that, acknowledging in *Communio et Progressio* that:

> A careful appraisal of the entire range of the communications media, a prudent and well-informed planning for pastoral work and in every apostolic enterprise, all this is the rightful province of the ecclesiastical authorities. They, in their turn, should depend upon the advice of experienced experts in the different branches of communication (CP 4).

Recognizing the limits of their expertise, the Church has shied away from enumerating the ingredients that go into skillfully developed media. She expects us to form our judgments on those questions according to the criteria laid out by those whose expertise really is camera angles or software design. We can find out more about those criteria by reading movie reviews and trade magazines. We can also simply pay attention to the design of popular websites or social media technologies. Media-makers put a great deal of time and money into researching what works, what reaches people, and what consumers expect, and the fruits of their research inevitably show up in their final product.

We also need to remember that the criteria change for what constitutes well-made media. What struck people as good cinematography in 1932 or as terrific special effects in 1955 would not pass muster today. The same holds true for new media. A well-designed, user-friendly website just three years ago looks different from a well-designed, user-friendly website today. That's another reason why, rather than issuing regular communiqués on what constitutes skillfully developed media at any given point in time, the Church simply urges Catholics to educate themselves about the media—to learn how to recognize and create media that meets the culture's expectations for what constitutes skillfully developed products (see CP 106–107).

In *Communio et Progressio*, noting that "forming Catholics as media and communications professionals is one of the priorities of the Church," the Church says that task belongs not only to those earning their living in the field, but also to all those who use media.

The well-trained recipient will be able to take part in the dialogue promoted by the media and will demand high quality in communications. Catholic schools and organizations cannot ignore the urgent duty they have in this field. These schools and institutions will take care to teach young people not only to be good Christians when they are recipients but also to be active in using all the aids to communication that lie within the media, now called the "total language." So, young people will be true citizens of that age of social communication, which has already begun (CP 107).

Those words were written in 1971, well before the advent of blogs, podcasts, and cell phones with built-in video cameras. Accordingly, they are mysteriously prescient, recognizing decades ago what is now a cultural truth: we all have the potential to be media-makers. It no longer takes a college degree, a paying job, or fancy equipment to make media. Today, anyone with a cell phone or Internet connection can make media, and anyone who has a Facebook page or a YouTube account can show the media they make to the world.

The Church not only urges us to take advantage of that opportunity, to "be active in using all the aids to communication that lie within the media," but to speak that language with knowledge. That means skillfully developed isn't just a key we use to evaluate the media we watch. It's a key that should exercise quality control over the media we make—over what we write on our blogs, post on our Facebook pages, or film for display on YouTube.

Whether we're designing a website for our family or giving input on the website design for our parish, the media we make should conform to the standards by which the culture judges and uses media. The quality of our content can never be an excuse for a lack of quality in our delivery of that content.

Separating the Wheat from the Chaff: Illustrating the Sixth Media Key

CATHOLIC HOLLYWOOD

Barbara Nicolosi's blog, "Church of the Masses," features a running list of the writer's favorite films. Nicolosi—a former Paulist sister turned Hollywood insider—titled the list, "It's Not All Garbage." The title is blunt but apt. Although skillfully developed films are a dime a dozen in Hollywood, skillfully developed films that are also compatible with a Catholic worldview are much rarer. It's not "all garbage," but it takes some work to find the gems.

Rarer still are skillfully developed films made from an explicitly Catholic point of view. All too often, movies about God, the Faith, or saints fall short of the film industry's (and the public's) standards for what constitutes a well-executed film. But "a well-made Catholic movie" doesn't have to be an oxymoron. It is possible to make great and critically acclaimed films that also happen to be deeply Catholic. Consider, for example, Mel Gibson's *The Passion of the Christ*.

Gibson set out to make a truly Catholic film, one filled with the riches of Scripture and Tradition, but one that also appealed to a wide audience. He wanted to make a great movie, not just a Catholic movie, and he wanted to make a movie that people actually saw. To do that, he knew he had to create a final product that was as well-made as anything else Hollywood puts out. In other words, he knew he had to meet the public's expectations for what a major motion picture should deliver.

To do that, Gibson spent millions of his own dollars and drew upon some of the most technically gifted craftsmen in the film industry. The end result was a film that grossed over $370 million domestically, with $125 million of that in its opening weekend. Not all who saw the film loved it—the violence was more than many could take—but they still saw it. The message Gibson wanted to get out—that Christ died an unimaginably terrible death for us—got out. And Hollywood commended him for the results. In 2005, the Motion Picture Academy nominated the movie for three Oscars—best cinematography, best makeup, and best original score. It also picked up another 17 wins and 10 nominations at other awards shows.

Along with the awards came praise from critics summarizing why the film garnered so many honors.

Claudia Puig of *USA Today* wrote, "Gibson has made a stunning film, beautifully photographed in contrasting dark and golden hues...." Roger Ebert of the *Chicago Sun-Times* explained, "I was moved by the depth of feeling, by the skill of the actors and technicians, by their desire to see this project through no matter what." And Chris Vognar of the *Dallas Morning News* said, "Controversy aside, [*The Passion*] is dramatically intense, skillfully constructed and often harrowing, in ways that should have an impact on people of any or no particular faith."[44]

Those are words of praise any moviemaker would proudly claim. But again, few explicitly Catholics films in recent years have met with the same degree of success—either at the box office or with critics. In some cases, that's simply because those movies didn't have the wide distribution and extensive marketing *The Passion* had (i.e. *Bella).* But in other cases, distribution and marketing problems were secondary issues. The real problem was that the films were less than skillfully developed.

That was unfortunately the case with the film *Thérèse: The Story of St. Thérèse of Lisieux.*

Thérèse's director, Leonardo DiFillipis, had the best of intentions. He wanted to create a beautiful and compelling film about one of the most beloved saints of all time. And, like Gibson, he wanted his film to appeal to more than just Catholics. He wanted people who had never heard about the Little Flower to fall in love with her and find in her a model to follow. But that didn't happen.

Grossing a mere $2.6 million in combined box office and DVD sales, the film was almost universally panned, even by many Catholics. Some of the choicer comments by reviewers included *Entertainment Weekly's* note that "Thérese unfolds with the sunlight-and-daffodils piety of a Sunday school slide show. . . ."; LA Weekly's advice was to "Skip the movie. Stay home, read the book and say three Hail Marys. . . ."; *The New York Times'* observation that "fluffy costumes and French location shoots are the only production elements that don't seem wholly amateurish. . . ."; and *The Chicago Reader's* belief that the movie "has the spiritual and emotional depth of a Hallmark card."[45]

Those remarks were justified. Where *The Passion* succeeded—with first-rate acting, scripting, cinematography, music, and editing—*Thérèse* failed. The storytelling felt at turns didactic and inadequate. Likewise, the acting came across as forced and the cinematography outdated. Even the soundtrack failed, at times seeming to have been lifted off of one of the cheesier episodes of *Little House on the Prairie.*

None of that is to say there weren't good elements in the film or that Catholics can't enjoy it for the story it tells. Catechetically, *Thérèse* has some merit. But cinematically, it doesn't. As the *National Catholic Register's* Stephen Greydenhaus acknowledged in his lackluster review of the film:

> Realistically, hopes of *Thérèse's* appeal reaching outside the believing world, or even outside the Catholic community, are unlikely to be realized. The film lacks the psychological depth and spiritual insight that attracts non-Catholics to *Story of a Soul.* [46]

Thérèse was never going to be the box office hit *The Passion* was. One of Hollywood's most influential actors and directors produced *The Passion.* A little known Catholic actor produced *Thérèse.* But despite that, *Thérèse* didn't have to be a critical disaster. Had it been more skillfully made, not only could it have garnered more space at the box office, but it could have done far more good for Catholics and non-Catholics alike. Because the quality of the film was compromised, so was its reach and power.

DIGITAL QUALITY CONTROL

Just as the culture brings expectations with it when it goes to the movies, it likewise brings expectations with it when it goes online. Today, people expect websites to be easy to read and easy to navigate. They don't want to see large, continuous blocks of text, and they do want to see video and audio podcasts, graphics, and hyperlinks to more information. They also want the ability to give feedback and talk with others. They expect interactivity. That's what they find when they go to the best and most popular secular sites on the Web, sites like Facebook, Wikipedia, Amazon, and Entertainment Weekly. That's also what they expect to find when they go to the websites of Catholic ministries and apostolates.

And oftentimes, they do.

Catholic websites such as Catholic Exchange, Catholic Answers, and Catholic Match attract significant amounts of Web traffic with their popular forums and chat rooms. The St. Paul Center for Biblical Theology's website, SalvationHistory.com, and Catholics United for the Faith's website, CUF.org, both feature online talks, lectures, and Bible studies. Popular Catholic bloggers Thomas Peters and Father John Zuhlsdorf regularly update readers via Twitter feeds, while EWTN and SQPN offer podcasts commenting on news, faith formation, and the culture. Even traditional Catholic news outlets such as *Our Sunday Visitor* and *The National Catholic Register* have developed a Web presence, taking portions of their print editions online and launching daily blogs featuring the opinions of their editors and writers.

Those websites are successful because their designers and contributors have mastered the language of the new media. They understand how social media can enhance their work, they know what people expect from them, and they've incorporated that understanding and those expectations into the form and function of their sites.

However, not all Catholic apostolates and organizations have been such quick studies. That point was made all too clear in 2010, when the Center for the Study of Church Management at Villanova School of Business released the findings of its nationwide study of Catholic parish websites.

According to the study, the vast majority of parishes surveyed maintain woefully inadequate websites. Although most do pretty well at the basics—96 percent list parish Mass times and 75 percent offer a link to the Sunday bulletin—few take advantage of user-friendly tools that can make life easier for both parish staff and parish members.

For example, only 12 percent post sacramental forms on their sites, and only 2 percent provide interactive forms that can be submitted online. Similarly, only 14 percent allow parishioners to sign up for events via the Web, while just over a third allow people to register at the parish online. Even something as simple as posting a calendar of parish events was done by little more than half of the parishes surveyed. Even fewer parishes have embraced new media tools such as blogs—only 10 percent of the parishes surveyed had one—and only 8 percent of parishes offered podcasts.[47]

Ironically, just weeks before the study was released, Pope Benedict XVI, in his 2010 World Communications Day Message, urged priests to embrace the Internet and "proclaim the Gospel by employing the latest generation of audiovisual resources (images, videos, animated features, blogs, websites). . . ."

As it turns out, that message was more than necessary.

Giving God Our Best:
Why Skillfully-Developed Media Matters

All too often, the phrase, "the soft bigotry of low expectations" comes a little too close to describing some Catholics' attitudes towards Catholic or Christian media. We're so happy to find Christian media—any Christian media—that we don't complain if it's not the most well-made film or video game on the block. We're so grateful that it presents truth and doesn't violate any major moral norms that we let the media-makers off the hook for any flaws in its overall quality. Basically, we expect less of it than we expect of secular media.

But when you expect less you get less. And "less" is not going to reach the people who need to be reached the most. It's not going to cut it outside of Catholic circles.

Almost forty years ago, the Church succinctly described that problem, noting in *Communio et Progressio* that:

> People today have grown so used to the entertaining style and skillful presentation of communications by the media that they are intolerant of what is obviously inferior in any public presentation (CP 130).

Having a great message does not let Catholic media-makers off the hook when it comes to craftsmanship. The Church expects Catholic media to be as well-made as its secular counterparts. And that's because like it or not, packaging matters. It increases credibility. It increases believability. It tells users and viewers that the media-makers know what they're doing.

It also captures and holds people's attention, which in this fast-paced, media-saturated culture, is no small task.

Ultimately, no matter how deadly or false the underlying message of a particular piece of media might be, if it comes in the right package—if it's been skillfully developed according to cultural expectations and industry standards—it will strike many people as good and true. Conversely, no matter how good and true the message of a badly developed piece of media may be, its goodness and truth will be compromised by its lack of quality. It will seem less believable, less true, less compelling.

It also will be less effective. Catholic parishes failing to develop good websites isn't just a good illustration of Catholic media that isn't well-made. It's a real problem for the Church right now.

In an interview following the release of the Villanova study, the lead researcher, Charles Zech, pointed out that, "As a Church, we need to be concerned [about the study results]. Things that most Catholics under forty take for granted, can't be found on parish websites. We're not doing all we can to connect with them, and that's a problem."

Zech went on to explain that this problem stems in part from the fact that as many as 80 percent of younger Catholics visit a parish's website before deciding whether or not to actually visit the church. If the website is difficult to navigate or fails to communicate a sense of the parish, many of those Web visitors might never become real visitors.[48]

On another level, outdated and inadequate websites are a problem because that means parishes aren't doing everything that can be done to spread the Gospel.

When younger Americans have questions about the Faith, the first place they go is to the Internet. Through blog posts, podcasts of homilies, and links to good Catholic content, parishes and other Catholic websites can help those searchers find the answers they're looking for.

But on countless Catholic websites—parish sites, diocesan sites, and organization sites—that isn't happening. The ministries and apostolates aren't paying heed to what constitutes skillfully developed media, and ultimately, that's compromising their ability to do their job. Which is unfortunate, as their job happens to be the most important job in the world.

If Catholics want to reach people through the media, we have to recognize what skillfully developed media is, learn from it, and produce it.

When we fail to recognize what constitutes skillfully developed media, we fail to incorporate the principles governing well-designed media into our own use. That failing could mean making bad recommendations about movies to friends—recommending well-intentioned but badly made films or television shows that will leave them with a negative impression of Catholic media. It also could mean creating blogs, videos, and websites that don't touch people, that don't reach people because the media isn't engaging, captivating, or compelling.

Again, in this day and age, we all can be media-makers. Most of us *are* media-makers in one form or another. And as such we have "a duty in conscience to make [our]selves competent in the art of social communication in order to be effective...." (CP 15).

Applying the Sixth Media Key

STEP 1: PRAY
Pray for the theological virtue of faith for yourself and for those working in the media industry.

> "Faith is the theological virtue by which we believe in God and believe all that he has said and revealed to us, and that Holy Church proposes for our belief, because he is truth itself. By faith 'man freely commits his entire self to God.' For this reason the believer seeks to know and do God's will" (CCC 1814).

STEP 2: RESEARCH

When reading movie reviews, pay attention to the praise movie reviewers give. Learn what they consider praiseworthy and why.

Visit websites designed by those with the money to research what people want and expect. The websites of secular news organizations and magazines, as well as political organizations, are a great place to start.

Occasionally and when it's not spiritually dangerous for you, watch the films that win Oscars and television shows that win Emmy's. Be familiar with what others consider skillfully developed media. Likewise, become familiar with the rating systems for movies and video games and recognize the limitations of these rating systems (e.g., their failure to consider context, purpose, and truth, the self-governing nature of current video game rating systems, etc).

STEP 3: ASK QUESTIONS

1. Am I willing to learn what makes media effective, develop the skills to use media effectively, and keep those skills up-to-date?

2. How would I rate the quality of the acting in a given film? The cinematography? The soundtrack? The editing? Other technical aspects of the film?

3. Is the storytelling compelling? Engaging? Well-written?

4. If it's a film or television program, does the media show a story or simply tell a story? Is it illustrative—making its point through engaging the viewer and revealing its objective through the characters' actions, or is it didactic—taking a heavy-handed approach and proselytizing through unnatural characterizations and story development?

5. Is the message accessible to its target audience? Is it in any way unclear or "over the audience's head"?

6. What tools and features do popular websites typically offer? What does that tell me about people's expectations and desires for the Web?

7. What makes a website easy to use and navigate? How much text is typically on each page of a website? How long are most videos? Podcasts?

8. What does this tell me about the ideal length of audio-visual media in different venues?

9. Does the site support two-way social communication and interactivity (e.g., online discussion forums, blogs, message boards, chat facilities, calendaring tools)?

10. What kinds of engaging, rich media content (e.g., animations, videos, podcasts, dynamically changing and updated material, interactive graphical user interfaces) are integrated into the site?

STEP 4: INTEGRATION

☛ Give specific critiques of how well-developed media is. Don't just say, "It's good" or "It's bad," but comment on the acting, writing, and technical aspects of the production, website, or media tool.

☛ Use what you learn about what constitutes skillfully developed media when you create your own media. If you have a blog, make it interactive, giving readers a space to comment. On your social networking page, post links to videos and music. And if you enjoy making videos for YouTube, keep them short, fill them with surprises, and add interactive links.

☛ Encourage your parish to have a Facebook or MySpace page, and volunteer to help monitor comments or discussions in chat rooms on the site.

☛ If a good Catholic movie is coming to a theatre near you, shell out the $10 to see it on the big screen rather than waiting to see it on DVD. Reward good filmmaking.

☞ With the increasing availability of tools for making media at home, try your hand at making a video or video game with the kids. Make it a fun family (or parish or catechetical group) activity, and spice it up with special effects and your own creativity.

STEP 5: PASSING IT ON

☞ Encourage an interest in media-making and an understanding of what makes for skillfully-developed media by:

☞ Enrolling high school-aged students in a summer course on photography, Web design, video game design, or filmmaking at local universities or colleges;

☞ Asking them the same questions you ask yourself about how well-made media is;

☞ Asking them to back up their critiques of media with specific reasons for their opinion;

☞ Encouraging them to watch classic and award-winning films, as well as movies and programming aimed at young people, so that they can assess the different levels of quality;

☞ Providing them with access to the tools they need to make media of their own when possible. This doesn't have to be expensive— freeware video and audio, and even video game-making tools all can be found online.

○━━

When secular media-makers fail to produce skillfully developed media, they're failing at the job that pays their bills. But when Catholics fail to produce skillfully developed media, we're failing to do all we can to preach the Gospel. We're also failing to glorify God by giving Him our best.

As Catholics, we need to appreciate, reward, and make skillfully developed media if we want to be "true citizens of that age of social communication." We also need to speak the "language" of the media so that we can recognize and create effective media, media that engages, communicates, and moves. And to do that, we can't just look to what constitutes well-made media. We also need to look to ourselves, the culture, and what media is capable of. We need to look to experience.

Chapter Eight

Motivated by and Relevant to Experience
The Seventh Media Key

A long time ago, man fell from grace. He rebelled against God and earned himself a one-way ticket out of Eden. His descendents followed suit, forsaking their birthright for a mess of pottage.

Despite man's ingratitude, insubordination, and insolence, God kept talking to him. He talked to man through floods and plagues and pillars of smoke. He talked to man through judges, prophets, and priests. And every once in awhile, He got through to someone. But those people were the exception, not the rule. Most people were too caught up in the world to listen to prophets . . . or even mysterious voices emanating from clouds.

God knew all along, of course, that it would take more than talking clouds to get man's attention. He knew there was ultimately only one way to get through to His selfish, stubborn, wayward children: the Incarnation.

God became man in order to pay the price for our sins. He took on flesh so that He could be the spotless lamb, the blameless offering. But He also became man so that He could talk to us. He became man so He could better communicate with us. He became man because that was the only possible way He could really and truly get through to us.

As man, Jesus Christ delivered the message of God's saving plan in a language we could understand. And not only did He deliver that message, He *was* the message. Jesus was God's saving plan. To paraphrase Marshall McLuhan: the medium was the message.[49]

In *Communio et Progressio*, the Church shows us how the Incarnation points the way to the seventh media key: all media should be motivated by and relevant to experience.

> While He was on earth Christ revealed Himself as the Perfect Communicator. Through His "incarnation," He utterly identified Himself with those who were to receive His communication, and He gave His message not only in words but in the whole manner of His life. He spoke from within, that is to say, from out of the press of His people. He preached the Divine message without fear or compromise. He adjusted to His people's way of talking and to their patterns of thought. And He spoke out of the predicament of their time (CP 11).

That's what it means to be relevant to experience. Media should take its cue from Christ and be rooted in the realities of the world we live in. It should take on familiar flesh and speak a language we know so that we can truly hear and understand the message it presents to us. It should reflect our experience of the human condition.

Communio et Progressio goes on to say:

> Communication is more than the expression of ideas and the indication of emotion. At its most profound level it is the giving of self in love. Christ's communication was, in fact, spirit and life. In the institution of the Holy Eucharist, Christ gave us the most perfect and most intimate form of communion between God and man possible in this life, and, out of this, the deepest possible unity between men (CP 11).

That's motivated by experience. When it comes to media, as it did in the Incarnation, the medium matters. Christ didn't just communicate a message—He communicated Himself. So too with media. There, the medium we use to communicate a message is also an integral part of that communication. Accordingly, media should reflect our experience of the media.* It should do what media is supposed to do: create a sensory experience—an experience that appeals to our senses—in order to move our emotions, shape our thoughts, and inspire us to action. The medium used should help accomplish the message objective.

Bridging the Gap:
Understanding the Seventh Media Key

RELEVANT TO EXPERIENCE

When Jesus moved through Judea and Galilee, teaching the gathering crowds, He didn't explain Himself or His message using scholastic theological formulas. There's a place for those, but it wasn't in the homes of tax collectors and Pharisees. It wasn't on the hills and shores where widows and laborers gathered. A technical discussion of the nature of the Trinity wouldn't have captured their attention. It wouldn't have engaged them. It wouldn't have meant anything to them. It was a reality seemingly separate from their simple lives of farming, cleaning, and fishing.

So Jesus didn't deliver theological treatises. He told stories. He talked about sowing seeds and finding a pearl of great price. He depicted heaven as a great wedding banquet. He described good and evil with images of wheat and chaff. And He illustrated the role of Christians in the world by comparing them to salt, light, and yeast.

Jesus drew on all that was familiar to first century Jews in order to get His message across. He made it relevant to them, to their lives, and to their

---

* "Today, much that men and women know and think about life is conditioned by the media; to a considerable extent, human experience itself is an experience of media" (Pontifical Council for Social Communicaton, Pastoral Instruction *Aetatis Novae,* February 22, 1992, no. 2).

world. He captured their attention with ideas and images that were familiar, and He used those ideas and images to make His point. And because of that, they heard Him.

John Paul II made note of this, writing:

> The Incarnate Word has left us an example of how to communicate with the Father and with humanity, whether in moments of silence and recollection, or in preaching in every place and in every way. He explains the Scriptures, expresses himself in parables, dialogues within the intimacy of the home, speaks in the squares, along the streets, on the shores of the lake and on the mountaintops (RD 5).

Jesus made His message relevant to the people of His day by speaking as they spoke, going where they gathered, and couching it in metaphors they could understand. Good media does the same.

It's accessible, understandable, and relatable. It gives us characters with depth, who resemble ourselves or people we know with all our hopes, dreams, strengths, talents, and quirks. It also places those characters in situations that, at their heart, are similar to situations we find ourselves in. It depicts authentic struggles and conflicts. And it offers resolutions to those struggles that illuminate the course we need to follow. Good media also does all that in a language we can understand. It uses words, metaphors, and images that make sense to us. Good media connects with us when it touches something in us, when it speaks to our own experience of need, love, fear, or want. It reflects the world as we know it back to us.

That doesn't mean, of course, that good media can't be imaginative. Fairy tales, fantasy, and science fiction can be rooted very much in experience. Remember what the Church tells us in *Communio et Progressio*:

Even when the artist takes flight from the tangible and solid world and pursues his creative fantasies, he can give priceless insight into the human condition. Stories fashioned out of imagination in which the artist creates characters that live and evolve in a world of fiction, these too communicate their special truth. Even though they are not real, they are realistic; for they are made of the very stuff of human life (CP 56).

The very stuff of human life—that's what makes for good media.

MOTIVATED BY EXPERIENCE

Media, however, doesn't just depict or correspond to our experience of life. Media itself is an experience because it gives us an experience. Through sights and sounds it creates a sensorial experience.†

A good suspenseful movie, with the right lighting, camera angles, and soundtrack, doesn't simply present to us a picture of a hero or heroine in danger. It actually causes our bodies to respond like we are in danger. Our hearts pound and our palms sweat. Similarly a video game uses graphics, sounds, narrative, and, increasingly, touch to immerse us in the action on the screen. Even a PowerPoint presentation, skillfully used, can create a sensorial experience. Slides featuring the layout of a battlefield or a recreated 3-D interactive fly-through of the temple in Jerusalem give life to a lecture on the Napoleonic Wars or ancient Israel. They stimulate and awaken our imagination, by first stimulating and awakening our sight.

We often don't think of media as an experience because it's an experience we have every day in a hundred different ways. It's how we live—immersed in media and affected by media. That's why it's helpful to step back and look at what came before this media age of ours.

---

† "Among the various technical arts which transmit the ideas of men, those occupy a special place today, as we said, which communicate as widely as possible news of all kinds to ears and eyes by means of sounds and pictures. This manner of spreading pictures and sounds, so far as the spirit is concerned, is supremely adapted to the nature of men, as Aquinas says: 'But it is natural to man to come to things of the understanding through things of sense; for all our knowledge has its origin in a sense.' [STh., I. q. 1, art. 9] Indeed, the sense of sight, as being more noble and more honourable than other senses, [STh., I, q. 67, a. 1] more easily leads to a knowledge of spiritual things. Therefore, the three chief technical methods of telecommunication, i.e. those of the Motion Pictures, Radio and Television, deal not only with men's recreation and leisure—though many who "listen-in" and view, seek this alone—but especially with the propagation of those subjects which, while aiding both mental culture and spiritual growth, can powerfully contribute to the right training and shaping of the civil society of our times" (Pope Pius XII, Papal Encyclical *Miranda Prorsus*, September 8, 1957, no. 1–3).

Broadly speaking, when it comes to social communications, there have been three distinct periods.

First, there was the oral age, the age before the printing press made the written word easily accessible. During this period, nearly all knowledge was communicated through seeing, hearing, and touching. It was an oral, visual, and tactile world. Knowledge was not so much analyzed as memorized. The most learned men and women weren't those who devised new ideas, but rather those who mastered ideas already known. And they mastered them not on their own, but in community, by associating with those who possessed the knowledge they sought. Learning, therefore, was not only sensorial—through the senses—but participatory. It required concerted and extensive interaction with others.

With the invention of the printing press, the literate age supplanted the oral age. In this period, knowledge was primarily communicated through the written word. And in order to communicate knowledge to others, a person had to develop linear, sequential thinking. They had to be able to explain themselves, one sentence at a time, in a clear and logical progression. The importance of the other senses was diminished. So was the importance of community. Learning via the written word meant one separated oneself from the group, doing one's most serious and intensive study alone in hours of quiet reading.

Over the past century, the literate age has rapidly given way to the media age. This age integrates the two ages that preceded it. Through media, sensorial experiences have again come to play a major role in how we acquire knowledge. We still learn through reading, but we also learn through watching, listening to, and interacting with media. Likewise, participation and community have again become integral to the passing on of knowledge. Discussion, debate, and talking ideas through with others play a greater role in classrooms, just as they do in online communities. The printed word still matters. It matters a great deal. But as media has become an increasingly important part of our culture, people have come to expect and depend upon more than the printed word to aid them in the learning process. They also want videos, interactive presentations, music, and forums where they can discuss and interact. [50]

So what's the point of all this theorizing? It goes back to what we talked about at the beginning of this chapter. When Jesus came to give men the Good News, He wasn't just delivering a message: He was the message. Similarly, the media doesn't just deliver a message. It's an integral part of the message. The medium matters. How well it corresponds to the age we're in—an age that learns through sensorial experiences, as well as the printed word—determines how effectively it delivers its message. If media isn't motivated by experience, if it doesn't give an experience of some truth, some event, some place, it's not carrying out its proper task.

Embracing the Media Age:
Illustrating the Seventh Media Key

BRINGING STORIES TO LIFE

In 2005, the classic children's tale, *The Lion, the Witch, and the Wardrobe*, finally became a major motion picture. For all sorts of reasons, the movie version of the book was an excellent piece of media—from the message it delivered to the skill with which it was made. We could probably use it to illustrate nearly every one of the seven media keys. But it's a particularly good example of a movie that is relevant to experience *and* motivated by experience.

The story is, of course, a fairy tale. The characters move within a world of imagination, a world of talking lions, evil witches, and centuries' old curses. And yet, it's still very much our world, populated by people very much like ourselves. When the young Edmund lies to his older siblings, refusing to admit that he had visited Narnia with his younger sister Lucy, most of us know all too well why he did it; ego and vanity, the desire to seem wiser than another, have led us into similar falsehoods. Most of us can also identify with little Lucy, whose siblings doubt her tales of

Narnia. Like her, those of us who've glimpsed the beauty and truth of Christ have also, at times, felt rejected and mocked by those who haven't seen what we've seen. Mr. Tumnus' fear of those who abuse their authority, Peter's frustration with Edmund's bad choices, Susan's desire to seem grownup and worldly—all those emotions, desires, and more resonate with us. They may be the emotions and desires of fictional children in a make-believe world. But they're our emotions and desires as well.

The characters in Narnia are relevant to our experience. So is the story. At its heart, *The Lion, the Witch, and the Wardrobe* isn't simply about four children who wander into a magical world. It's about sin and its consequences. The world of Narnia was cursed with a hundred years of winter because of a sin committed shortly after its creation. And a sin committed by Edmund—the betrayal of his brother and sisters to the White Witch—leads to the death of Aslan. Narnia's Lion King gives his life in exchange for Edmund's. He dies to pay the price for Edmund's sin. In this fallen world, that's an awfully familiar story.

As media, the movie succeeds because it's relevant to human experience. It also succeeds because it gives us an experience. The enchanted world, which was once seen only with the eyes of readers' imaginations, becomes a visible reality on screen. Fawns with red umbrellas, talking beavers, and evil dwarfs walk before us. The struggle between good and evil also comes to life, with music and sound effects, not to mention computer-generated imagery, tight editing, and plenty of fancy camera work, all helping viewers feel as if they're experiencing Narnia's great thaw, the flight from the White Witch, and the movie's climactic battle sequence right alongside the characters on screen. Through media, Narnia becomes more than just a world to be read about. It becomes a world to be experienced.

Where Narnia succeeds is where the movie, *Thérèse: The Story of St. Thérèse of Lisieux*, failed. St. Thérèse of Lisieux was one of the greatest saints of all time. But she wasn't born with a halo on her head. Deeply wounded by the death of her mother, Thérèse was, in many ways, a spoiled and selfish child given to fits of petulance and self-pity. Later, in the Carmelites, she struggled greatly with the strict penances proscribed by the order. She also endured long periods of spiritual dryness and doubt. That's the woman we encounter in her autobiography, *The Story of a Soul*. And that woman, for all her great sanctity, is eminently relatable.

But the Thérèse of the 2004 film is more a Victorian nursery image of the saint than the flesh and blood creature who struggled even as she grew in holiness. Little of the struggle and darkness that transformed her into an extraordinary saint makes it onto the screen—only small flashes of temper or tears, only a few words spoken about doubt. The end result is a character who is not relatable, who is as different from the rest of us fallen human beings as night from day. She isn't relevant to us.

Nor do we walk away from the film feeling as if we've journeyed with Thérèse through darkness. The movie tells rather than shows the saint's spiritual journey, with the actress who portrayed Thérèse saying in a voiceover, "Jesus has permitted my soul to be invaded by a thick darkness." But we never *see* her soul being invaded by a thick darkness. We don't watch Thérèse progress through a dark night. We don't experience the graces of her conversion or the struggles of her spiritual purgation because the film doesn't give us an experience of them.

THE INTERACTIVE EXPERIENCE

One of the reasons for the success of blogs is that the writers, in commenting on the culture or the news of the day, also give glimpses into their own lives. The best blogs are relatable blogs. They say something about the writer—about who they are, where they've been, and what matters to them. From mentions of travel plans and children's names to anecdotes about their day, personal details woven into commentary help the blogger build a relationship with his readers. They become knowable, relatable. And because of that, what the writer has to say becomes more compelling and their message seems more credible.

In the Catholic world, early bloggers such as Amy Welborn and Mark Shea mastered that art, becoming two of the most popular Catholic blogs on the Web with thousands of visitors every day. Readers knew about their children, their struggles with faith and family, even their favorite television shows. And they listened to what Welborn and Shea had to say about the Faith, at least in part, precisely because of that.

The Web not only allows readers to "know" writers such as Welborn and Shea, it also gives readers, via videos, pictures, and sounds, a sensorial experience, and encourages interaction and participation through comment boxes and forums. Through appealing to the senses and people's desire for community, interactive multimedia websites move the emotions and work through multiple means to encourage learning.

Recognizing this has led many major media outlets to change how they structure their websites. Gone are long blocks of text and links to PDF's. Gradually, media institutions like *National Review Magazine* or Fox News, as well as Catholic apostolates such as Catholic Answers and Catholic Exchange, have added to their websites blogs, video podcasts, forums in which users can debate current issues, and polls where they can register their opinions. They've become virtual community centers filled with familiar personalities and a host of new media activities to engage users' eyes and ears as well as their hearts and minds.

When websites don't do that, however, when they rely solely on large chunks of text or links to even more text or text-dense PDFs, their creators are acting like we still live in the primary literate age. They're not giving people a sensorial experience. They are, in fact, under-using media. And accordingly, their creations are less effective.

Getting the Message:
Why the Seventh Media Key Matters

FOR MEDIA-MAKERS

For those making media, it's important that what they make is relatable, accessible, and understandable if they actually want their media to accomplish its intended end. No matter how good or true the message behind the media might be, if people don't feel like they can relate to or understand the story being told or the information presented, the message won't reach them. It won't move them or inspire them to action.

Remember, in today's world, almost all of us, to some extent, are media-makers. We have Facebook pages, blogs, and participate in online forums. We put videos up on YouTube or film podcasts for our friends. We talk online about our work, our politics, and our faith. We interact with others via media, even if it's only via email. And as we interact in virtual communities, it's important to remember to keep what we're saying relevant. If we want to reach people, we need to write or talk clearly, not speaking above our audience, and, when appropriate, integrating some element of the personal into what we say and do. If we want to be effective communicators, we need to be relatable communicators. We need to connect with people on the level of personal experience.

This is doubly true if we're talking about the Faith. When we are using media to preach the Gospel, our attitude needs to be more that of a witness than a teacher.

In his book, *The Evangelization Equation*, Father James Wehner describes the place of personal experience and witness in teaching the Faith, noting:

> Whether you're dealing with teens or adults, they want to
> see two things: 1) That you truly believe what you teach and
> act according to those beliefs, and 2) That those beliefs and

actions make a difference in your own life. They need to see those things for a host of reasons. Partly because we live in a consumer culture. Everyone is selling something, and before we buy, we want to know if the goods are genuine. We also want to know if they will benefit us. That applies to the Catholic faith as much as it does to the Apple iPhone 3G. . . .

Post-modernism has also made witness matter more. When everything is relative, when authority is always to be questioned, experience still holds sway. When people can see that like them you've struggled, but that you've found answers and help in those struggles through the faith, that answers what the best apologetics can't.[51]

That advice is as true for evangelizing through the media as it is for evangelizing face-to-face. The seventh media key serves as an important reminder that telling and showing how God is working in our lives is a more powerful introduction to the Faith in this media age—which values learning through community and participation—than launching into an abstract theological treatise.

Likewise, whether we're blogging about the Faith online or teaching students in a classroom, we need to use media as it was meant to be used—as a tool to give a sensorial experience. When we do that, it makes whatever we're talking about or whatever lesson we're presenting more effective.

Nearly fifty years ago, reflecting on how media was changing learning, Marshall McLuhan proposed that light coming through a medium had the power to capture our attention with an almost hypnotic intensity. According to McLuhan, long before the invention of the television or computer, that power manifested itself in stained glass windows. Rather than just hanging up paintings of the saints or the mysteries of the Rosary, churches had those images rendered in multicolored glass and set in stone walls. As light poured through those windows, they became more powerful aids for meditation. They captured people's attention in ways mere paintings could not.[52]

Today, computer screens and televisions work in a similar way, capturing and holding our attention. Think for example of how difficult it can be to focus on the person sitting across from you in a restaurant, when a television is on just behind their shoulder. Even though you want to look at the person, it's hard to pull your gaze away from the images on the screen.

Media offers us the opportunity to harness that power and use it to educate, enlighten, and transform. But we can only harness that power when we recognize that power. That's what the seventh media key helps us to do.

FOR MEDIA CONSUMERS

Even if you never have and never will make a piece of media in your life, the seventh media key still matters. And it matters because of what it tells us about our culture, ourselves, and our children.

People love what they can relate to and they seek the experiences they desire. That's true regardless if we're eight or eighty. So just as media-makers use the seventh media key to make good media, we can use it as a gauge to assess what's important and not important to others and ourselves.

In other words, what we love says a great deal about who we are. What we can relate to, what we find understandable and accessible, what experiences we seek, reveal something about us. That's true on a cultural level: *American Idol's* ratings say as much about our culture's obsession with fame and celebrity as *The Bachelor's* ratings say about our obsession with sex. It's also true on a personal level: one woman's preference for the BBC's Jane Austen movies and another's preference for Jennifer Lopez flicks reveals something about each woman. And it's especially true about our children: if our children want to watch the *American Pie* movies or play *Grand Theft Auto*, that tells us something about what they or their peers are thinking about and doing (or getting ready to do). If it's *High*

School Musical or *Disney Camp Rock* that's capturing their attention, that tells us something else.

When used as a lamp to illuminate the desires and fears that attract us to media, the seventh media key can become a guide for parents seeking to understand their children. It also can become a guide for each of us as we struggle to know our culture and ourselves better. Without that self-knowledge, we can't overcome all the struggles and weaknesses holding us back from holiness. And without that knowledge of our culture, we can't reach out to it, engage it, and help heal it. The seventh media key, like media itself, is a tool for engagement and evangelization.

Applying the Seventh Media Key

STEP 1: PRAY

Pray for the theological virtue of charity, which can promote sympathy for and understanding of others.

Charity, the *Catechism* says, "is the theological virtue by which we love God above all things for his own sake, and our neighbor as ourselves for the love of God . . . The practice of all the virtues is animated and inspired by charity, which . . . upholds and purifies our human ability to love, and raises it to the supernatural perfection of divine love . . . charity demands beneficence and fraternal correction; it is benevolence; it fosters reciprocity and remains disinterested and generous; it is friendship and communion" (CCC 1822, 1827, 1829).

STEP 2: RESEARCH

To find out the audience a movie is intended for, view the trailers shown before the film or at the beginning of the DVD. Trailers are almost always chosen for one or two target audiences. You can also confirm this by watching the directors' commentaries available on most DVDs.

To find out the same about a television show or website, pay careful attention to the advertising during commercials or in banner and pop-up ads.

Likewise, it's often true that the protagonist of the show, commercial, or advertisement represents the demographic that the media-makers hope to target.

STEP 3: ASK QUESTIONS

1. Who is the target audience of the media? To whom does it aim to be relatable?

2. Can I relate to this film/TV show/game? If so, in what ways do I relate to it?

3. Are the characters in a film, show, or game believable? Who do I find myself relating to the most? Why?

4. What story is the media trying to tell? Have I seen aspects of that story played out in real life?

5. How does the conflict in a game or show resolve? Is that resolution believable?

6. Does this media immerse me in the events taking place on screen? Do I feel like I'm there? If yes, why?

7. In my own use of the media, do I use all the tools available to me to give people a sensorial experience, therefore enabling them to understand me better?

8. Do I understand the difference between the oral, print, and media ages? How does my own use of the media reflect that understanding?

9. How does my own use of the media give people an experience of God and the Church?

10. How can I imitate Christ in my attempts to communicate with people?

STEP 4: INTEGRATION

- Reflect on why certain pieces of media appeal to you or the culture and assess whether its appeal is healthy or unhealthy.

- Embed short YouTube videos on your blog or social networking page. These videos should add the dimension of sensorial experience to ideas you're discussing.

- Don't use media in a presentation for work or school just for the sake of using media. Only use it if it complements your oral presentation, enriching the content with a sensorial experience and not distracting from it with too much written text, either in hand-outs or Power-Point slides.

- Incorporate stories about yourself and your life into your blog, even if the topic is faith or politics. Let yourself be known through the media that you use, so that those reading the media have a sense of you and your credibility. Be the lamp (or lampstand) Christ calls you to be (Lk. 11:33–36).

- Share your conversion story or faith journey via your blog or a social networking page.

STEP 5: PASS IT ON

- Ask your children the same questions you ask yourself about media.

- Talk to your children about what their favorite movie/show/game/band is. Watch it, play it, or listen to it. Then, without expressing an opinion, ask them what it is about the media that appeals to them.

- Ask them what their friends' favorite movies, games, and music are, and why they like them so much. (This works especially well if they won't tell you what their favorites are. Usually the two are one and the same.)

☞ Ask them who they think the media-makers want to appeal to and what they do to make their media appealing to their target audience.

☞ Don't permit video games in the house that immerse your child in an experience of violence, crime, and sexuality.

☞ When it comes to learning and research, encourage them to rely not only on media for learning, but to go to the library to check out and read books. Remember, part of media's job is to engage and inspire, then point us toward textual information that—in part because of the effort reading and thinking require—can promote contemplation.

Conclusion
Without Fear

Once more, media is a tool. It's an instrument that "can be used to proclaim the Gospel or to silence it within men's hearts" (AN 4).

It's also a tool that, according to Pope Paul VI, the Church "would feel guilty before the Lord if she did not utilize. . . ." (EN 45).

Reflecting on that last statement, Pope John Paul II wrote:

> In fact, the Church is not only called upon to use the mass media to spread the Gospel but, today more than ever, to integrate the message of salvation into the "new culture" that these powerful means of communication create and amplify. It tells us that the use of the techniques and the technologies of contemporary communications is an integral part of its mission in the third millennium (RD 2).

Those are strong words, on all counts. A very serious and very difficult challenge lies before us. The Church asks us to take up this tool and wield it with the utmost precision. That precision is required because the stakes are so very high. Eternal life with God is one outcome. Eternal separation from God is another. Ultimately, our use of the media will help lead us (and others) to one of those two destinations. In the end, there is no eternal in-between. There's heaven and there's hell.

With stakes like that, God hasn't left us to navigate our way through the media age we find ourselves in alone: "Believers in Christ know they can count on the help of the Holy Spirit," John Paul wrote in "The Rapid Development" (RD 13).

We also have the seven media keys—clear guiding principles that can help us separate the wheat from the chaff in media and use media in the right ways for the right ends.

If we rely on these keys, we can approach media with balance and with an awareness of the attitudes underlying it. We can use media to help men and women become more fully human, to illuminate and proclaim truth, and to inspire people towards their transcendent destiny. And we can do that when media is not only true and just, but when it's skillfully developed, relevant to human experience, and motivated by a desire to give people a sensorial experience through media.

These are the principles the Church has given us and continues to reassert.[53] For now, there seems to be no more and no less. Depending on our relationship to the media—whether we are teachers, parents, writers, news producers, filmmakers, or simply consumers—the ways we apply these keys will differ. Balance will mean something a little different to a news reporter—who's tasked with giving equal weight to multiple viewpoints and bringing the plights of minorities or underrepresented demographics to light—than it will to the mother of a six-year-old boy. Likewise, using the media to inspire will look different on the blog of a Catholic writer than it does on the homepage of ESPN. But in essence, the keys remain the same regardless of who applies them.

They also remain the same whether we employ them to evaluate our own use of the media or to evaluate the merit of the media we're consuming.

In some ways, it might help to think of the seven keys as a rating system for both. Media that is balanced, made with the right attitude, respects the dignity of the human person, proclaims truth, is skillfully developed, and motivated by and relevant to experience, earns seven virtual stars. We can earn the same seven stars when we approach media with balance and awareness, when we use it to promote human dignity, spread truth, inspire ourselves and others, and when the media we make is well-made, rooted in human experience, and gives a sensorial experience. In both applications, all seven keys serve as a gauge—an indicator of whether we should be watching or using certain forms of media and a measurement of whether something in our own media behavior needs to change.

Finally, the seven media keys remain the same regardless of whatever new and exciting developments in technology the coming years will inevitably bring. Very soon, one social networking site will give way to another. New ways of communicating will merge. New technologies will come on the market. But the seven keys won't change. They are our media constants, core principles as true in 1965 as they were in 2005 and as they will be in 2565. If we remember them and use them, we will always be able to safely navigate our way through the ever-changing media jungle.

Baptism: Remembering the Means and the End

Using these keys may at times be a challenge. We're human, and the temptation to jettison good guides and follow bad ones is ever-present. But remembering the keys is actually quite easy. If you abbreviate a few of the keys, you get the following:

Balance

Attitude

Person

Truth

Inspires

Skillfully Developed

Motivated by and Relevant to Experience

Then, if you take the first letter of each key, you get a word: Baptism. That mnemonic device has made it easy for my students to always remember the seven media keys. After all, in a certain sense, that's exactly what Christians are called to do with and to the media. We're called to "baptize" the culture with media, entering into it, engaging it, and bringing it to life in Christ through the tools it relies on. We're also called to baptize media itself, filling it with a respect for truth and justice, and transforming it into a tool that can be used to proclaim the Gospel and lead people to God.

The tools we've been given really are "gifts from God." And we mustn't hesitate to use them as God has asked us to use them. We mustn't be afraid.

'The People of God walk in history," *Communio et Progressio* reminds us. As such, we should "look forward with confidence and even with enthusiasm to whatever the development of communications in a space age may have to offer" (CP 18).

In the end, however, it's always more about us than it is about the tools. Shortly before his death, John Paul II urged us to not be afraid of the obstacles—real and virtual—the world presents to us: "Do not be afraid of being opposed by the world! Jesus has assured us, 'I have conquered the world!' (Jn. 16:33)."

He then added:

> Do not be afraid even of your own weakness and inadequacy! The Divine Master has said, "I am with you always, until the end of the world" (Mt. 28:20). Communicate the message of Christ's hope, grace and love, keeping always alive, in this passing world, the eternal perspective of heaven, a perspective which no communications medium can ever directly communicate. ...(RD 14).

John Paul reminds us there that it's us, real people with real bodies, who are ultimately responsible for bringing people to Jesus. And no technology, no matter how wondrous, can ever take our place. Human interaction, human conversation, human love—that's the ultimate medium for communicating Christ. Each of us is a far greater gift and a much more marvelous thing than any piece of media. Each of us can do far more good than the Internet, and each of us can image the truth and beauty of God far more completely than any film or video game, no matter how realistic or immersive it may be. After all, we're the ones who earned a "very good" at Creation, and we're the ones whom media exists to serve.

Remembering that and believing that can be a greater challenge than remembering and believing in the wonders of technology. But if we can manage to do that, we can manage an iPhone. If we can keep a true understanding of who we are at the heart of all our interactions with media, then we can manage to use media responsibly and use it well, free of fear, free to play, free to make our way to the Great Communicator Himself.

Appendix

Church Documents on Media and Social Communications: A Timeline

By 2009, 61 documents, not counting the many ancillary communiqués, had been issued by the Church.

Year proclaimed	Name of social communications document/milestones in the development of the Pontifical Council for Social Communications	Type	Author
1936	*Vigilanti Cura* (with "Vigilant Care")	Encyclical letter	Pope Pius XI
1948	Establishment *ad experimentum* of the Pontifical Commission for the Study and Ecclesiastical Evaluation of Films on Religious or Moral Subjects		
1948	Establishment (with name change) of the Pontifical Commission for Educational and Religious Films		
1952	Name changed to Pontifical Commission for the Cinema		
1954	Name changed to Pontifical Commission for the Cinema, Radio and Television		
1955	*The Ideal Film* (Exhortations of His Holiness Pius XII to Representatives of the World of the Cinema)	Exhortation	Pope Pius XII
1957	*Miranda Prorsus* ("Very Remarkable")	Encyclical letter	Pope Pius XII
1958	*Clarius explendescit* (proclaims Saint Claire as Heavenly Patron of Television; French language)	Apostolic letter	Pope Pius XII

Appendix

Year Proclaimed	Name of Social Communications Document/Milestones in the Development of the Pontifical Council for Social Communications	Type	Author
1959	*Boni Pastoris* (the office "of the Good Shepherd")	Apostolic letter *Motu Proprio* ("by his own initiative")	Pope John XXIII
1959	The Commission for the Cinema, Radio and Television is made a permanent Office of the Holy See		
1963	*Inter Mirifica* ("Among the Marvelous Things")	Conciliar decree	Pontifical council
1964	Transformation of the existing Commission for the Cinema, Radio and Television into the Pontifical Commission for Social Communications		
1967	Church and Social Communication: First World Communication Day	1st World Communications Day message	Pope Paul VI
1968	*Social Communications and the Development of Nations*	2nd World Communications Day message	Pope Paul VI
1969	*Social Communications and the Family*	3rd World Communications Day message	Pope Paul VI
1970	*Social Communications and Youth*	4th World Communications Day message	Pope Paul VI
1971	*The Role of Communications Media in Promoting Unity Among Men*	5th World Communications Day message	Pope Paul VI
1971	*Communio et Progressio* ("Unity and Advancement")	Pastoral Instruction	Pontifical council
1972	*The Media of Social Communications at the Service of Truth*	6th World Communications Day message	Pope Paul VI
1973	*The Mass Media and the Affirmation and Promotion of Spiritual Values*	7th World Communications Day message	Pope Paul VI
1973	*An Appeal to All Contemplative Religious*	Council document	Pontifical council

Year proclaimed	Name of social communications document/milestones in the development of the Pontifical Council for Social Communications	Type	Author
1974	*Social Communications and Evangelization in Today's World*	8th World Communications Day message	Pope Paul VI
1975	*The Mass Media and Reconciliation*	9th World Communications Day message	Pope Paul VI
1976	*Social Communications and the Fundamental Rights and Duties of Man*	10th World Communications Day message	Pope Paul VI
1977	*Advertising in the Mass Media: Benefits, Dangers, Responsibilities*	11th World Communications Day message	Pope Paul VI
1978	*The Receiver in Social Communications; His Expectations, His Rights, His Duties*	12th World Communications Day message	Pope Paul VI
1979	*Social Communications: Protecting the Child and Promoting His Best Interest in the Family and in Society*	13th World Communications Day message	Pope John Paul II
1980	*Social Communications and Family*	14th World Communications Day message	Pope John Paul II
1981	*Social Communications and Responsible Human Freedom*	15th World Communications Day message	Pope John Paul II
1982	*Social Communications and the Problems of the Elderly*	16th World Communications Day message	Pope John Paul II
1983	*Social Communications and the Promotion of Peace*	17th World Communications Day message	Pope John Paul II
1984	*Social Communication: Instruments of Encounter Between Faith and Culture*	18th World Communications Day message	Pope John Paul II
1985	*Social Communications for a Christian Promotion of Youth*	19th World Communications Day message	Pope John Paul II
1986	*Social Communications and the Christian Formation of Public Opinion*	20th World Communications Day message	Pope John Paul II

Year proclaimed	Name of social communications document/milestones in the development of the Pontifical Council for Social Communications	Type	Author
1986	*Guide to the Training of Future Priests Concerning the Instruments of Social Communication*	Council document	Congregation for Catholic Education
1987	*Social Communications at the Service of Justice and Peace*	21st World Communications Day message	Pope John Paul II
1988	*Social Communications and the Promotion of Solidarity and Fraternity Between Peoples and Nations*	22nd World Communications Day message	Pope John Paul II
1989	*Religion in the Mass Media*	23rd World Communications Day message	Pope John Paul II
1989	The Pontifical Commission for Social Communications is made into an Office of the Roman Curia in its own right, becoming the Pontifical Council for Social Communications		
1989	*Pornography and Violence in the Communications Media: A Pastoral Response*	Council document	Pontifical council
1989	*Criteria for Ecumenical and Inter-religious Cooperation in Communications*	Council document	Pontifical council
1990	*The Christian Message in a Computer Culture*	24th World Communications Day message	Pope John Paul II
1991	*The Communications Media and the Unity and Progress of the Human Family*	25th World Communications Day message	Pope John Paul II
1992	*The Proclamation of Christ's Message in the Communications Media*	26th World Communications Day message	Pope John Paul II
1992	*Aetatis Novae* ("A New Era")	Pastoral Instruction	Pontifical council
1993	*Videocassettes and Audiocassettes in the Formation of Culture and of Conscience*	27th World Communications Day message	Pope John Paul II
1994	*Television and Family: Guidelines for Good Viewing*	28th World Communications Day message	Pope John Paul II

Year PROCLAIMED	NAME OF SOCIAL COMMUNICATIONS DOCUMENT/MILESTONES IN THE DEVELOPMENT OF THE PONTIFICAL COUNCIL FOR SOCIAL COMMUNICATIONS	TYPE	AUTHOR
1995	Cinema: Communicator of Culture and of Values	29th World Communications Day message	Pope John Paul II
1996	100 Years of Cinema	Council document	Fr. Virgilio Fantuzzi
1996	The Media: Modern Forum for Promoting the Role of Women in Society	30th World Communications Day message	Pope John Paul II
1997	Ethics in Advertising	Council document	Pontifical council
1997	Communicating Jesus: The Way, the Truth and the Life	31st World Communications Day message	Pope John Paul II
1998	Sustained by the Spirit, Communicate Hope	32nd World Communications Day message	Pope John Paul II
1999	Mass Media: A Friendly Companion for Those in Search of the Father	33rd World Communications Day message	Pope John Paul II
2000	Ethics in Communication	Council document	Pontifical council
2000	Proclaiming Christ in the Media at the Dawn of the New Millennium	34th World Communications Day message	Pope John Paul II
2001	Preach from the Housetops: The Gospel in the Age of Global Communication	35th World Communications Day message	Pope John Paul II
2002	The Church and Internet	Council document	Pontifical council
2002	Ethics in Internet	Council document	Pontifical council
2002	Internet: A New Forum for Proclaiming the Gospel	36th World Communications Day message	Pope John Paul II
2003	The Communications Media at the Service of Authentic Peace in the Light of Pacem in Terris	37th World Communications Day message	Pope John Paul II
2004	The Media and the Family: A Risk and a Richness	38th World Communications Day message	Pope John Paul II

Appendix

Year proclaimed	Name of social communications document/milestones in the development of the Pontifical Council for Social Communications	Type	Author
2005	The Communications Media: At the Service of Understanding Among Peoples	39th World Communications Day message	Pope John Paul II
2005	The Rapid Development	Apostolic letter	Pope John Paul II
2006	The Media: A Network for Communication, Communion and Cooperation	40th World Communications Day message	Pope Benedict XVI
2007	Children and the Media: A Challenge for Education	41st World Communications Day message	Pope Benedict XVI
2008	The Media: At the Crossroads between self-promotion and service. Searching for the Truth in order to share it with others	42nd World Communications Day message	Pope Benedict XVI
2009	New Technologies, New Relationships: Promoting a Culture of Respect, Dialogue and Friendship	43rd World Communications Day message	Pope Benedict XVI
2010	Priests Stand at the Threshold of a New Era	44th World Communications Day message	Pope Benedict XVI

Endnotes

Note: All URLs are current as of April 2010.

INTRODUCTION

1 These terms were originally coined by Marc Prensky in an article entitled "Digital Natives, Digital Immigrants," *The New Horizon*, Vol. 5, No. 9 (West Yorkshire, UK: MCB University Press, 2001).

CHAPTER ONE

2 Cindy Kranz, "Nude Photo Led to Suicide," *Cincinnati Enquirer* (March 22, 2009), http://news.cincinnati.com/article/20090322/NEWS01/903220312.

3 Brian Stelter, "8 Hours a Day Spent On Screens, Study Finds," *The New York Times* (March 26, 2009), www.nytimes.com/2009/03/27/business/media/27adco.html; Lee Raines, "Internet, Broadband, and Cell Phone Statistics," Pew Internet and American Life Project (January 5, 2010), www.pewinternet.org/Reports/2010/Internet-broadband-and-cell-phone-statistics.aspx; The Marist Poll, "Cell Phone Nation" (June 12, 2009), http://maristpoll.marist.edu/612-cell-phone-nation/; Nielsen, "2010 Media Industry Fact Sheet" (February 2, 2010), www.blog.nielsen.com/nielsenwire/press/nielsen-fact-sheet-2010.pdf; Amanda Lenhart, "Teens and Sexting," Pew Research Center Publications (Dec. 15, 2009), www.pewresearch.org/pubs/1440/; Shawn Oliver, "Internet Use On the Up and Up—Is Anyone Surprised?" *Hot Hardware* (December 24, 2009), www.hothardware.com/News/Internet-Use-On-The-Up-And-UpIs-Anyone-Surprised.

4 David Finkelhor, Kimberly Mitchell, Janis Wolak, "Unwanted and Wanted Exposure to Online Pornography in a Sample of Youth Internet Users," *Pediatrics*, Vol. 19, No. 2 (American Academy of Pediatrics, February 2007), 247–57.

5 Dale Kunkel, Keren Eyal, *Sex on TV 4* (Kaiser Family Foundation, November 5, 2005), 21. Available at www.kff.org/entmedia/7398.cfm; Norman Herr, "Television and Health Statistics," www.csun.edu/science/health/docs/tv&health.html.

6 Tori DeAngelis, "Web Pornography's Effect on Children," *Monitor*, Vol. 38, No. 10 (American Psychological Association, November 2007), 50; Media Awareness Network, "Research on the Effects of Media Violence," www.media-awareness.ca/english/issues/violence/effects_media_violence.cfm; Parents Television Council, "TV Bloodbath: Violence on Prime Time Broadcasts" (2003), www.parentstv.org/PTC/publications/reports/stateindustryviolence/exsummary.asp; Rebecca L. Collins, Marc N. Elliott, Sandra H. Berry, David E. Kanouse, Dale Kunkel, Sarah B. Hunter, and Angela Miu, "Watching Sex on Television Predicts Adolescent Initiation of Sexual Behavior," *Pediatrics* Vol. 114, No. 3 (American Academy of Pediatrics, September 2004), 280–89.

7 Mark Bauerlein, *The Dumbest Generation: How the Digital Age Stupefies Young Americans and Jeopardizes Our Future* (New York, NY: Penguin, 2008), 11–38.

8 ACT, "Rigor at Risk" (May 2007), 1. Available at www.act.org/research/policymakers/reports/rigor.html.

9   Bauerlein, *The Dumbest Generation*, 113–14; Emily Stimpson, "Can Teens Stay Connected Without Losing Touch?" *Our Sunday Visitor* (June 14, 2009), http://www.osv.com/tabid/7621/itemid/4948/Can-teens-stay-connected-without-losing-touch.aspx.

10 The study was conducted by Cyber Sentinal and reported on the website of *The Telegraph* in February 2009. The data is available at www.telegraph.co.uk/technology/4574792/Teenagers-spend-an-average-of-31-hours-online.html.

11 Mark Edmunson, "Dwelling in Possibilities," *The Chronicle for Higher Education*, Vol. 54, No. 27 (March 14, 2008) B7.

12 Bauerlein, vii-xi.

13 Edmunson, ibid.

14 Stimpson, ibid.

15 Emily Stimpson, "Closing the Book on Reading," *Our Sunday Visitor* (August 31, 2008), www.osv.com/tabid/7621/itemid/3972/Closing-the-book-on-reading.aspx.

16 Nicholas Carr, "Is Google Making Us Stupid?" *Atlantic Magazine* (July/August 2008), www.theatlantic.com/magazine/archive/2008/07/is-google-making-us-stupid/6868/.

17 Maggie Jackson, *Distracted: The Erosion of Attention and the Coming Dark Age* (Amherst, NY: Promethus Books, 2008).

18 Emily Stimpson, "Author Distills the Importance of Attention," *Our Sunday Visitor* (October 11, 2009), www.osv.com/tabid/7621/itemid/5464/Author-distills-the-importance-of-attention.aspx.

CHAPTER TWO

19 Here, the word "porn" pejoratively refers to the extensive graphic depictions.

20 Amanda Lenhard, "Teens and Mobile Phones Over the Past Five Years: Pew Internet Looks Back," Pew Internet and American Life Project (August 2009), http://authoring.pewinternet.org/Reports/2009/14--Teens-and-Mobile-Phones-Data-Memo.aspx.

21 Stimpson, "Can Teens Stay Connected Without Losing Touch?"

22 See www.netaddiction.com and Jesse Jiang, "Inside China's Fight Against Internet Addiction," *Time* (January 26, 2009), www.time.com/time/world/article/0,8599,1874380,00.html.

CHAPTER THREE

23 Collins, et. all, 2004; http://www.media-awareness.ca/english/issues/violence/effects_media_violence.cfm.

24 Gallup 2008 poll, "Gay and Lesbian Rights," http://www.gallup.com/poll/1651/gay-lesbian-rights.aspx.

25 Dan Gilgoff, "Catholics the Same or More Liberal than Others on Moral Issues," *U.S. News & World Report* (March 30, 2009), www.usnews.com/blogs/god-and-country/2009/03/30/gallup-poll-catholics-the-same-or-more-liberal-than-others-on-moral-issues.html.

26 John Paul II, Message for the 32nd World Communications Day *Sustained by the Spirit, Communicate Hope* (May 24, 1998), 19. Available at www.vatican.va/holy_father/john_paul_ii.

CHAPTER FOUR

27 Some of the more notable "cyber-bullying" suicides include 13-year-old Megan Meier in 2006, 12-year-old Sarah Butler in 2009, and 15-year-old Phoebe Prince in 2010. For more information see www.makeadifferenceforkids.org; Sophia Van, "Colleges Fight Back Against Anonymous Gossip Sites," *Time* (December 7, 2009), www.time.com/time/magazine/article/0,9171,1942971,00.html.

28 Jake Halpern, *Fame Junkies* (New York, NY: Houghton-Mifflin, 2007), 38.

29 See: Edmunson, ibid.; Matt Labash, "Down with Facebook," *The Weekly Standard* (March 16, 2009), www.weeklystandard.com/Content/Public/Articles/000/000/016/256implp.asp; Emily Stimpson, "How to Steer Clear of Pitfalls When Using Facebook," *Our Sunday Visitor* (April 19, 2009), www.osv.com/tabid/7621/itemid/4709/How-to-steer-clear-of-pitfalls-when-using-Facebook.aspx; Emily Stimpson, "Revolution," *Franciscan Way* (Winter 2010), 12–17.

30 Kristin Kalning, "Is a virtual affair real-world infidelity?" MSNBC.com (April 16, 2007), http://www.msnbc.msn.com/id/18139090/wid/11915829.

31 Olivia Barker, "Technology Leaves Teens Speechless," *USA Today* (May 29, 2006), http://www.usatoday.com/tech/news/techinnovations/2006-05-29-teen-texting_x.htm; Stimpson, "Can Teens Stay Connected Without Losing Touch."

32 Baucklin, 113-14

CHAPTER FIVE

33 Originally cited in Pius XII, *Allocution given on October 28, 1955 to the patrons of the art of the cinema gathered in Rome for their International Convention*, A.A.S. XLVII (1955), 822–23.

34 Stimpson, "How to Steer Clear of Pitfalls When Using Facebook."

35 Jayati Chaudhuri, "Deterring Digital Plagiarism: How Effective is the Digital Detection Process," *Webology*, Vol. 5, No. 1 (March 2008), http://webology.ir/2008/v5n1/a50.html.

36 Emily Stimpson, "The Good, the True, and the Beautiful," *Franciscan Way* (Winter 2009), 22–23.

37 Joanie Farley Gillispie and Jayne Gackenbach, *Cyber Rules: What You Really Need to Know About the Internet* (New York: NY: Norton & Company, 2007), 24.

CHAPTER SIX

38 Stephen Cox, *It's A Wonderful Life: A Memory Book*, (Nashville, TN: Cumberland House Publishing, 2003), 11.

39 Ted Bridis, "Kentucky School Shooting May Have Been Inspired By Violent Movie," *The Day* (December 4, 1997), 36.

40 See C.A. Anderson, L. Berkowitz, E. Donnerstein, L.R. Huesmann, J.D. Johnson, D. Linz, "The Influence of Media Violence on Youth," *Psychological Science in the Public Interest, Vol. 4, No. 3* (2003), 83. Although some have argued that the consumption of violent video games hasn't given rise to a general increase in societal violence, we cannot conveniently ignore any long-term links between cumulative, habitual exposures to violent video games and aggression, simply because such studies are lacking, or because of a concern that we're not going to sell an additional 500 copies of _____ (name your video game company's best-selling title here).

41 E.F. Schneider, A. Lang, M. Shin, & S.D. Bradley, "Death with a Story: How Story Impacts Emotional, Motivational, and Physiological Responses to First-Person Shooter Video Games," *Human Communication Research*, Vol. 30, No. 3 (2004), 361–75.

42 Bioware, the developers of the computer game *Mass Effect*, made, at least to a certain extent, an attempt to integrate 'morality' into the game play, with 'significant' repercussions that were dependent on the choices the player made with the character played. Yet here too, morality was limited to whether one acted professionally as a military soldier with a mission, or as a ruthless renegade with a take-no-prisoners approach.

43 Pontifical Council for Social Communications, *The Church and the Internet* (February 22, 2002), 5. Available at www.vatican.va/roman_curia/pontifical_councils/pccs.

CHAPTER SEVEN

44 See RottenTomatoes.com (Rottentomatoes.com/m/passion_of_the_christ).

45 See MetaCritic.com (http://www.metacritic.com/film/titles/therese).

46 Stephen Greydenhaus, "Thérèse: The Story of St. Thérèse of Lisieux," DecentFilms.com (2004), www.decentfilms.com/reviews/therese2004.html.

47 Emily Stimpson, "How Parish Websites Can Better Connect with Catholics," *Our Sunday Visitor* (March 14, 2010), www.osv.com/tabid/7621/itemid/6084/How-parish-websites-can-better-connect-with-Cathol.aspx.

48 Stimpson, ibid.

CHAPTER EIGHT

49   Marshall McLuhan, *Understanding Media: The Extensions of Man,* 1994 edition (Cambridge, MA: The MIT Press, 1964), 7.

50   I owe much of the work here to Catholic author, teacher, thinker, and pop-icon luminary Marshall McLuhan, as well as to his student Fr. Walter Ong, a prominent author, teacher, and scholar in his own right. Taken together, their work postulates that there are three predominant periods describing the development of speech, writing, print, and media technology. They also discuss the powerful influence of media on society and culture. The three predominant periods they describe are 1) The primary oral, 2) The primary literate, and 3) The electronic age (which I'm referring to as the media technology age).

51   Rev. James Wehner, *The Evangelization Equation: The Who, the What, and the How of the New Evangelization* (Steubenville, OH: Emmaus Road Press, forthcoming).

52   Paul Levinson, *Digital McLuhan: A Guide to the Information Millennium* (New York, NY: Routledge, 1999), 9.

CONCLUSION

53   For example, in Pope Benedict XVI's encyclical letter *Caritas in Veritate,* three of these media keys appear in one sentence. There the pope tells us that to be effective, the tools of social communication should "focus on promoting the dignity of persons and peoples, they need to be clearly inspired by charity and placed at the service of truth" (June 29, 2009), 73. Available at http://www.vatican.va/holy_father/ benedict_xvi/encyclicals/documents/hf_ben-xvi_enc_20090629_caritas-in-veritate_en.html.

Endorsements for
Infinite Bandwidth

A very helpful guide to a very important but difficult issue: How do Catholics relate to the media explosion? Eugene Gan offers a thoughtful and constructive analysis, which is sure to illuminate and guide.

—Scott Hahn, PhD, internationally renowned
author and biblical theologian

In the exceptionally well-written and researched *Infinite Bandwidth*, Eugene Gan presents the reader with a comprehensive Catholic framework to consume and critique contemporary media. He skillfully argues that it is critical for Catholics to engage contemporary culture, using Pope John Paul II's comparison of today's new media landscape to the Areopagus—the social and intellectual hub of ancient Athens where Paul preached to pagans.

—Derry Connolly, PhD, president of
John Paul the Great Catholic University

Engaging and thoughtful as all media should be, Dr. Gan practices what he preaches in his book *Infinite Bandwidth*. He skillfully summarizes over seventy years of Catholic teaching on the marvels and menace of media and offers an engaging reflection as well as a helpful approach to media use for parents and teachers alike. If you are looking for a Catholic guide in this age of shifting values and the proliferation of the communication tools, *Infinite Bandwidth* is a tremendous resource.

—Father Robert P. Reed,
president of The CatholicTV Network

Some things take experience. Some things take a dad. And other things take a university professor. And some things must take all three. Eugene Gan has drawn on his experience as a user and creator of all sorts of media, his concerns as a father, and his understanding of the way college students live with their ever-present electronics to create a book that answers questions (and worries) that many Catholics may have had in the back of their minds for a long time. Unplugging across the board is not an option the Church recommends. I commend Eugene Gan highly for a well-crafted work that I am going to refer to often and recommend broadly.

—Sister Anne Joan Flanagan, Daughters of St. Paul,
popular writer and speaker

Infinite Bandwidth is a great gift to the Church. Dr. Gan masterfully pulls together the many Church documents and statements on media through the years. From those he gives seven media keys to help people properly critique all forms of media. He makes clear that we must not run in fear from the latest technologies and new forms of media, but we should embrace them with a critical eye and use them well for proclaiming the truth and beauty of our Catholic Faith. This book will change the way you view your next movie and listen to that new song. It will change the games you play on your computer and the apps in your iPhone.

—Father Jay Finelli, popular blogger and
podcaster at iPadre Catholic Podcasting